COHERENCE

How Telling the Truth Will Advance Your Cause

(and Save the World)

COHERENCE

How Telling the Truth Will Advance Your Cause

(and Save the World)

Richard H. Bailey

To TJ

Contents

A Good Place to Start

1. I love stories and metaphors. Consider yourself fairly warned.

2. What you are about to read is true.

3. Unless you are new to the marketing profession, you have my permission to skip or skim Chapter 2. It lays the foundation for the principles of coherence—and it's important—but my guess is that it is full of information you already know.

4. Occassionally, you'll find illustrations to intentionally support your reading. I encourage you to write notes in the margins, take time to answer the questions, record your responses and fill in the blanks. You may not be able to judge a book by its cover, but a book with your notes in the margins is probably a very good thing.

5. This book would not have been written without my wife and business partner, Tammy. She's actually the one who pushed to launch our agency on April 15, 1991 (tax day in the midst of a different difficult economy). That should tell you a bit of her optimism and

entrepreneurial spirit. She's spunky, creative and deliberate. We often say she's the one with her feet on the ground and I'm the one with my head in the clouds. Together, we just hang on to each other and make a great team. She's been "encouraging" me to write this for some time. I can never thank her enough.

6. I am grateful for the cheerleading and support of my favorite Millennials, Nick and Ashley and Nick's spouse, Lauren. They know I've been working on this for some time. They've known the obstacles. But they've never doubted its completion. And they've been great motivation to get it done. I love being their dad.

7. Cindy Harris provides a great example of personal coherence. I'm grateful for her encouragement, counsel and gentle critique. Dr. Greg Sipes inspires me. Great conversations, long car rides together and his own books sparked my thinking. I want to co-author a book with him. I think it makes perfect sense to pair a psychologist with a marketing guy. And he's really smart. For one thing, he married Markine, who has likewise been tremendously supportive. It's all about relationships, after all.

8. I intend that this book pays tribute to Lissa Hunt. Lissa was a copywriter at RHB from June of 1994 to July of 2003. She left us for the only job she said would take her away: being editor of her alma mater's alumni magazine. And Indiana University called. Lissa's custom was to listen to me rattle on about concepts and ideas and then abruptly run to her office, shut the door, and emerge a bit later with language that was magic on paper. She drafted two white papers with me that are reflected throughout this book and serve as the foundation of these premises. My dear friend's life was cut alarm-

ingly short by cancer in 2005 at the age of 42. I miss her as though she was family. Indeed, she was.

9. No man is an island and I am grateful for the whole continent that is Richard Harrison Bailey/The Agency. The RHB team comprises brilliant professionals—past and present—whose creativity, ingenuity, prowess and pure genius inspire me every day. Their collective talents are orchestral; their collective personalities, symphonic. Everyone who has been a part of RHB has been a part of this book. I am particularly grateful for the dedicated input, collaborative encouragement and careful editing of Dr. Meg Barrett and Ryan Millbern, two of the best writers with whom I've had the privilege to work. Meg instrumentally reworked a draft when she could tell I was really tired of editing and rewriting. It was the boost I needed at that moment. I am also indebted to straight-shooters Sam Waterson and Gail Straus who, partly because they are so "up" on everything, challenge my thinking and energize my ideas. Senior Art Director Kerry Prugh designed the cover and layout of this book; Brian Ross added his illustrations and infographics. Thanks to everyone.

10. Deep thanks go to Bob Spatig (University of South Florida); Andrea Cook (Warner Pacific College); Nancy McDuff (University of Georgia); and Betsy Mulenfield and Ken Huus (Sweet Briar College). Not only were they willing to let me tell their stories, they added their own perspectives to the content of this book. Further, they committed time to reading drafts of the book to ensure its integrity and contribute improvements. I am also grateful for the counsel, insight and investment from the "early" readers of book drafts in addition to all those above: Kerry Temple (University of Notre Dame),

Ken Anselment (Lawrence University), Mary Ellen Anderson (Indiana University), and Rae Goldsmith (CASE).

11. This book was written for and because of our clients. They have all challenged us with *their* challenges, inspired us to do our very best work and engaged us in their powerful and meaningful causes. Whether they are educating, healing, helping, serving or enlightening, each of them is improving the world in which we live. We are so proud of their efforts and so honored to help them succeed.

12. I used to work on a college campus as a fund-raiser, public relations manager and an admissions director (sometimes all at the same time). I am exceedingly grateful to two college presidents—Elwood Voller and Kenneth Coffman—and my first boss, David Gines, who saw a mustard seed of potential in me and who were willing to entrust me with decision-making authority that far exceeded my knowledge and capability at the time. My early professional experiences laid a track-tested foundation that opened the door to a lifetime career of serving other institutions with noble missions. I cannot thank them enough—as well as my exceptional professors and colleagues at Spring Arbor University—for the education they provided on all fronts.

13. The language throughout this book has been tested for its "teachability" on hundreds of outstanding students in my classes at the University of Notre Dame. To each of these future marketing marvels—the next generations of thinkers and doers—I wish to say "thank you." Through classroom discussions, your papers, your presentations and your questions, you've provided me a great education. Change the world with what you know.

14. So many great people have encouraged me along the way and for every nod, thumbs up, suggestion and word, I am most grateful. Many thanks to Jeff Crook; Julianne Butler; Jen Lowe; Laura Polian; Ron Mahurin; my coach Mary Miller, Todd, Ken, Dan, Mike, Tom, Phill and the rest of my SC cohort; David Baker; Arloa Sutter; my other sisters Jenny and JC; my MOOB colleagues Marcia, Marcia, Ed and John; and to everyone who has ever even hinted to me that I could write a book.

15. Though they are no longer here to receive my thanks, I wish to honor Floyd G and Betty F. Bailey for a lifetime of lessons in love that undergird the principle of coherence.

16. My friends call me Rick. You can call me Rick.

COHERENCE

How Telling the Truth Will Advance Your Cause
(and Save the World)

Introduction

By the time you are finished reading this book (assuming you finish it in the next day or so), it's likely that millions of high school students will have given thought to their college futures; millions of adults will consider returning to the classroom (though this time around it may look more like a computer monitor); millions of donors will have considered making a gift to their alma maters; and thousands of legislators and government employees will have focused attention on decisions related to higher education policy. So read quickly. You'll want to implement ideas in this book as fast as you can. What you read in these pages can make a difference for you and your institution.

Whether you are at the top of the higher-ed food chain or struggling as a bottom feeder,

...whether you enroll thousands or scores,

...whether you are dependent on tax dollars or a handful of dedicated benefactors,

...whether your next class determines your existence or whether your endowment will keep you buoyed forever,

this book can make you stronger, better and healthier.

Maybe even wealthier.

That's a big claim. But I believe it, because we've watched the principles in this book transform institutions. And, at the very least, the ideas here have helped dozens of colleges and universities achieve goals they had dreamed about.

For nearly twenty years, my colleagues and I have been on an important mission: We help great causes succeed. We have worked with more than 200 not-for-profit organizations of all shapes and sizes, helping them find their true selves, tell their wonderful stories and achieve their marketing ambitions.

In our work at Richard Harrison Bailey, we focus on the marketing and communication needs of higher education. And this book draws from our experiences with colleges and universities around the world. Along our journey, we've also been invited to work with other not-for-profit groups, since many of the principles we have developed apply to arts organizations, museums, associations, membership organizations, churches, hospitals and health-care providers, social justice agencies and professional services.

But this book isn't about us. It's about you—and your great cause. This isn't a marketing textbook, though it is full of important lessons learned from real-world experience. It's not based on data from a single scientific study, though the content stems from substantial qualitative and quantitative marketing research, including thousands of hours of interviews and listening. It's intended for practitioners more than theorists, though both are welcome readers.

If you are reading this and you are not interested in higher ed marketing, that's okay. The ideas will work for you, too. Some people have told us that these principles relate to their personal lives and their families, as well.

In this book, we'll introduce you to a strategy for achieving a greater sense of coherence between your organization and your customers. But you should know right now: It's not always an easy process. Unfortunately, despite many promises, there are no silver bullets for good marketing. There's not a website, technology, data management system or media outlet that will single-handedly "fix" your particular problem. But these chapters will give you the tools you need to join the journey to coherence. Our intent is to make the ideas we've tested and learned become a practical resource for you. We hope you will read along and say, "We should have done that. Hey! We *can* do that!"

Most of all, we hope that by telling our story, and the stories of our clients, you'll become even more excited about your own. You do indeed have a great cause. What you do every day—even when it seems mundane, and especially when you feel you can't go on like you are—is vitally important. You have the privilege of improving a life, expanding a horizon, elevating a possibility, giving hope, realizing promise, and yes, extending love.

Interested in thinking differently about your great cause?

Coherence is the discipline of ensuring a transparent connection between customer expectation (brand) and authentic user experience. Coherence is aligning what we deliver with what we say we deliver. Coherence engages customers in shaping a meaningful experience that meets their needs.

Coherence is telling the truth.

CHAPTER 1

The Revolution Begins

On a Tuesday afternoon in late September, 2002, we started a revolution at RHB.

We were sitting around the conference-room table, discussing our growing concern for our clients who were challenged and confused about branding. Everything we were seeing and reading suggested that brands were in trouble. Books, newspapers and magazines all reported on trends of shifting consumer behavior—in particular, a rapidly growing level of consumer empowerment. We tracked similar patterns among the consumers served by our clients. And while we were confident that we were serving our clients well, at least to the best of our abilities, we sensed that we could do and should do more. Our clients needed a new kind of relief: a better understanding of themselves in a consumer-driven world, and a way to connect with their consumers in new and more meaningful ways.

Clients were asking us the wrong questions. Consumers—especially young students and their families—were demanding more answers. Expectations for service and customer care were at all-time highs.

As we discussed the dilemmas our clients were facing, you could see and hear the passion for a solution. We had been making some significant "paradigm shifts" (that was the hot descriptor at the time) in our service to clients. While we offered award-winning creative solutions to our clients, we also provided new ways of thinking about brands and informed counsel about consumer interests.

Given the success of our clients, we knew we were on the right track. We had introduced some unique processes that helped our clients come to terms with their identities, strengths and distinctive points of differentiation. We employed proprietary research methods to unearth hidden gems that facilitate rich storytelling.

But how could we help our clients see that our approach was different? That what we were doing went beyond branding? And what do we call something that doesn't yet have a name?

I challenged our team to find a word or phrase that suggested honesty, transparency and authenticity. A word that helped convey the power of consumers with the integrity of performance and delivery on promises. A word that would suggest that conversation and dialogue were better tools in a connected world than advertising ever would be again.

We were thinking hard. Which meant it was quiet. And then a bit of magic broke the silence.

"Coherence?"

Spoken with that upward lilt that evokes a question—part Valley-speak, part timidity—Sam Waterson, our young, Californian, former-intern-turned-full-time-account manager, read Webster's definition:

> 1. *logically or aesthetically ordered or integrated :* **consistent** *<coherent style> <a coherent argument> b: having clarity or intelligibility :* **understandable**

And then we all grinned.

Coherence. Consistent and understandable.

And with a single word, the revolution began.

We had no intention of changing the world. Ours was not a political agenda. Nor were we motivated by religious fervor (though we were indeed passionate). "Control" and "power" were not watchwords, but we certainly anticipated empowering change. We wanted to turn our agency into the most effective, most helpful team we could be. And those we wanted to help were our clients: colleges, universities, fraternities and sororities, hospitals, foundations, associations, arts organizations, museums, churches and social service agencies. We wanted to help them find themselves, their voices and their wonderful places in the world. We wanted them to succeed in their great causes.

...

In the coming chapters, you'll encounter true examples and stories drawn from our work with scores of colleges and universities nationwide. But we'll periodically return to four institutions, in particular. One is a flagship public university. One is a single-gender private college. One is a church-related liberal arts college. One is a burgeoning newcomer.

Each of these four institutions has a lot going for it. Each has a great cause, a great purpose and a compelling mission. They are good at what they do. And they offer something distinctive in their markets. But they all came to our firm with specific needs. They weren't where they wanted to be. They needed some help—a map—to get to their destinations. Yet, they all had important questions that needed to be answered before they could even begin to make the journey.

How does a forward-looking campus come to terms with a difficult past?

In recent years, the University of Georgia has emerged as one of the elite public institutions not only in the Southeast, but also the nation. Having made significant strides in academic quality, and offering premier research, study abroad and honors programs, the institution was clearly on an upward trajectory.

To continue its forward momentum, UGA cast new goals. As the flagship institution of its state, UGA sought to enroll not only a well-qualified and academically prepared student body, but also one that reflected the population of its home state, Georgia. For UGA, this meant an incoming class that reflected a broader range of ethnic and racial diversity, as one measure. As another measure, it needed to attract students from all corners of the state, rather than limited geographic pockets. At the same time, to underscore the

University's position in the national education arena, UGA pictured a greater population of students from around the country and the world. And in all cases, it hoped to continue increasing its academic profile by enrolling high-achieving students who would make the most of the University's exceptional opportunities.

Thus, a destination was set: UGA was seeking a path of both selectivity and accessibility. Standing in the way, however, was its reputation, among many key constituents, for being inhospitable to minority students and uninterested in students from certain parts of Georgia. Long-held, and deeply rooted in specific events from the past, these perceptions meant that the University had some work to do before it could continue moving forward. Given the constraints of the past, how would UGA grow into its new vision for the future?

How does a college with a narrowing market connect with best-fit students?

Sweet Briar College, a 700-student women's college located in the foothills of Virginia's Blue Ridge Mountains, boasts many strengths, including an excellent liberal arts curriculum, a close-knit campus community, exceptional study-abroad and equestrian programs, and a gorgeous, 3,250-acre campus.

Nevertheless, Sweet Briar also faced several challenges—most notably, the increasingly difficult "sell" of a single-gender education.[1] In an effort to deepen its pool of prospective students, Sweet Briar had developed recruitment communications that downplayed the College's distinctive charms and quirky (even "girly") appeal, and instead focused on broad-level benefits—such as strong academic programs, internship opportunities and professional preparation— that would interest the widest audiences possible.

Despite these efforts, Sweet Briar continued to have difficulty connecting with the dwindling numbers of students willing to attend a single-gender institution. In order to sustain the integrity of the College, at least two changes needed to occur: Sweet Briar needed more funding, and it needed enrollment to grow and stabilize. Trustees examined all their options, including admitting men. In fact, several of Sweet Briar's closest competitors were choosing the co-ed route.

Sweet Briar determined a different course, opting to remain a women's college—a decision that reaffirmed the institution's original mission, and reflected a conviction that the one-of-a-kind education Sweet Briar offers continues to be both desired and needed by certain segments of the college-going population. But the challenge was clear: How would Sweet Briar reach them?

What does a college in the city look and feel like?

Warner Pacific College in Portland, Oregon, enjoys a wide range of strengths and assets—including its passionate, dedicated faculty and staff, a long-standing relationship with the Church of God (Anderson), and a distinctive general education curriculum that encourages students to wrestle with the notion of paradox.

Yet Warner Pacific faced a number of challenges. Financial short-falls hindered the College from maintaining its strong programs and stature in the market. Leaders were challenged by the campus' land-locked location at the foot of Mount Tabor (an extinct volcano in the Portland city limits). This urban setting was not perceived as an asset, when most of the College's successful competitors were in suburban settings. In fact, trustees were looking at new property and considering a campus move. A revitalized and growing adult-student program offered glimmers of hope, but the campus community showed signs of fatigue and low morale. Research with users— students and alumni—suggested the mission and vision weren't connecting with the experience.

Aware of these significant issues, campus leaders, including the president and senior officers, charted a course for change. Beginning with a clear articulation of mission, they shaped a vision—a desti- nation—that included a balanced budget, refreshed or new facilities, increased enrollments and a revitalized community of students, faculty and staff. And that vision took shape on the existing property.

With this destination set, leaders began asking difficult questions regarding coherence: How does an urban campus look, feel and act? What must change in terms of programs and offerings? In terms of accessibility and underserved populations? In terms of pricing?

How does a young institution find its place on the map?

Though the University of South Florida jumped in the higher education waters just over 50 years ago, it has certainly made a big splash. Unlike the other three institutions we've introduced, USF, when it retained RHB, wasn't necessarily facing some specific, glaring predicament. It was enrolling satisfactory numbers of students. It wasn't in danger of shutting its doors. It was ambling along adequately, but not with clear focus.

Nevertheless, as an ambitious youngster, USF set its sights on achieving more. It sought to strengthen the academic profile of its incoming classes, as well as to enroll more multicultural and out-of-state students. It aspired to improve freshman-to-sophomore retention rates. It wanted to shed an outdated reputation for being a "commuter school." And ultimately, it envisioned being ranked among the top 50 research universities in the United States—though when you're pitted against competitors two, three and even four times your age, finding elbow room at the table can be a formidable challenge. How does a relative newcomer to the higher education arena carve its niche in a very crowded market?

...

By using the strategy of coherence, we were confident we could answer these challenging questions. We knew we could help these schools succeed.

And succeed they did.

- In just one year, UGA experienced a 98 percent increase in enrollment deposits from African-American students, and a 24 percent increase in deposits from all multicultural students.

- In the first three years of our work for Sweet Briar, total applications for admission increased by 45 percent and enrollment increased by 28 percent; alumni and donors responded with enthusiasm.

- In two years at Warner Pacific, the number of full-time equivalent students jumped by more than 25 percent; within four years, the student population more than doubled; and neighbors increasingly engaged with the campus in meaningful ways.

- And our work with the University of South Florida yielded a 57 percent increase in applications, an 18.5 percent increase in African-American student enrollment, and a 15-point jump in average SAT scores—in just the first year. Further, with focus on student success, retention jumped to a remarkable 86 percent.[*]

...

This book is about the revolution of coherence. The concepts in these pages have revolutionized our firm. They've revolutionized our clients that employ them. And they can revolutionize your organization, too.

If you'd like to join the revolution, read on.

---

1 The first women's college was chartered in 1836; by the early 1960s, more than 300 women's colleges were in operation. By 2009, fewer than 50 single-gender women's colleges remained.

[*] The National Center for Higher Education Management Systems (NCHEMS) reports that the national average for freshman to sophomore retention at public institutions in 2008 was 76.8%; Florida's publics retained on average 73.6% (Source: NCES, IPEDS Enrollment Survey)

CHAPTER 2

Using the "B" Word

Not long ago, when websites were first being considered as instruments for marketing, I was seated next to a university president in a website planning meeting. In those days, presidents often commandeered those meetings since IT departments weren't fully developed, and most college campuses still hadn't identified who the official keepers of the sites would become. Shockingly, this wasn't that long ago.

During our meeting, when it was my turn to speak, I suggested to the planning committee that they consider the contribution the website would make in reflecting their brand. At the mention of that last word, the president turned sharply in my direction and said, "We don't use the 'B' word here." Recoiling, I asked, "What word do we use?" And his reply, properly informed by one of my competitors, was "Promise." Not a bad definition. A brand *is* a promise, in that a brand reflects a consistency in delivery of an expectation. I like that.

But I didn't particularly like that we couldn't use the word "brand." It's a great word. Yet, at the time (and maybe yet today on your campus), "brand" or "branding" was obviously associated with corporate or product-driven marketing in a way that can be repulsive to not-for-profit institutions—particularly colleges and universities—whose lofty missions are considered as rising high above mere "products." That's unfortunate, because brands are simply audiences' commonly held perceptions about a product or service that suggest repeatable expectations. And who among us doesn't want to ensure that our audiences have accurate perceptions and expectations of us?

...

Do you know Marty Neumeier? If not, you should. At least read his books. And visit his website. I use *The Brand Gap*[1] as required reading for my advertising students at the University of Notre Dame. They are dismayed to discover that he has encapsulated an undergraduate marketing degree in about 125 pages, particularly when they consider that they have just invested more than $100,000 to acquire the same volume of knowledge. So, if you could get football tickets *AND* read his books, you'd have a great college experience.

In *The Brand Gap*, Neumeier outlines an excellent history of the evolution of advertising. He reminds us that at the turn of the 20th century as new inventions and mechanization brought new products to the market, the focus was on features. As more products were introduced, we shifted to benefits. By the 1950s, the marketing focus shifted to the experience and feelings. And, by the turn of the

21st century, the work of marketing turned to identification and sense of belonging to a tribe of product or service "user groups."

Let's augment Neumeier's timetable with some marketing strategy-markers beginning in the 1930s and 40s. As more and more products were introduced to the market and as consumers consequently had more choices to make, the effort of marketing forced advertisers to work on matters of differentiation. As new features were added to existing products, the message of advertising turned to advantages of these features. In the 1950s, advertising turned to the relationship of these features to lifestyle. (Think how much we focused on the Cleavers as the quintessential American family.) By the 60s and 70s, as products and services became increasingly commoditized, consumers required shortcuts to identify their favorites. Al Ries and Jack Trout wrote their tome, *Positioning: The Battle for Your Mind* [2] from their articles in *Advertsiing Age* in the early 1970s, helping us all to understand how we rank products and services on little mental ladders. With signature examples like 7Up® and Avis®, Ries and Trout provided great insight that paved the way for greater attention to brands. Through the Reagan and Clinton years of more robust economies, consumers and, in turn, marketers elevated the importance of brands by integrating the total experience with particular products and services. Branding was in full force.

But then something truly remarkable occurred. Just like Gutenberg's printing press revolutionized the world in 1439, the introduction of consumer access to the Internet in the mid 1990s* transformed everything we understood about and practiced

---

* While the Internet was first introduced in the late 1960s, in terms of significant and easy consumer access, the integration of Microsoft® software with the Web in 1998 really catapulted the shift I'm speaking of here.

related to marketing strategy. Suddenly (and that word is chosen purposefully here), everything about branding shifted.

Until the Web became a part of everyday life for consumers, branding was managed and controlled by the "brander"—that is, the "owner" of the brand sort of called the shots. Brands were "controlled" by companies, organizations and institutions. The Web transferred that control from companies to consumers.

Branding has never been the same.

...

Let's back up. This is important.

You do not own your brand. You didn't even create your brand. The people who purchase your product, use your service or engage in your experience created your brand. Those consumers have shaped what you call your "brand."

You know the ol' "I wish I had a dollar for every time...?" Well, I wish I had a buck for every time we've heard from prospective clients something like this: "We need you to give us a brand." Or, "We're calling to see if you will 'brand' us." Or, "Can you help us find a brand?"

My response is always the same: *"I'm sorry. We can't do that."*

"Really? You can't?"

"Really. We can't."

"Why not?"

"Because you already have a brand."

"Uh...no, we don't. We're the best kept secret in (insert name of any state or region of the county here)."

"Really? Why do you suppose that is?"

"Because we don't have a brand."

"I'll bet you dinner that's not why."

"Really? You're on."

"Well, now you have to buy me dinner. Because the problem isn't that you don't have a brand. You simply have a brand you don't care for."

"Oh."

As much as I'd like to hand over a brand on a silver platter, our agency or any other agency cannot provide a brand. We can't. Because we do not make brands. Consumers make brands. Their encounters and experiences with you, proven over time, build and shape opinions and perspectives that define your brand.*

Your brand is the set of expectations associated with your industry and your particular delivery on those expectations. If you are a plumber, your brand includes the belief that you will fix leaky faucets, stop running toilets and repair damaged pipes. You will deliver expertise on moving water from one place to the next. Your brand also includes a perception that you will arrive or leave with messy hands and low-riding, rear end-exposing jeans. Your brand includes an expectation that you will arrive on the job late and your professional service will cost more than the estimate.

While a history of encounters with plumbers creates a certain set of general expectations from consumers, each plumber has the opportunity to differ from others in the set at various levels of

---

* *Your brand may be weak due to indifference or little name recognition, but you still have a brand that is defined by those who know you, though they indeed may be relatively few.*

performance delivery. Plumber A may choose to differentiate by always arriving with clean fingernails and well-fitting khakis. Plumber B may choose to consistently arrive on time. Plumber C may offer the lowest price. With consistent delivery on these features/benefits, consumers will come to expect "cleanliness" from Plumber A, "promptness" from Plumber B, and "bargain" from Plumber C. Though the plumbers each choose their own path of differentiation, based on their assessment of the heart of consumer need, over time, it is the consumers shaping the brand expectation.

If you are a college or university, your brand includes the consumers' confidence that you will teach enlightening classes that will help students achieve certain life goals: a life-sustaining and gratifying job, entrance to graduate school, satisfaction of earning a degree, greater salary and/or a better, more enjoyable life. It includes expectations for good instruction and support from faculty, excellent service from student development teams, well-working and efficient facilities, and a host of other services and experiences to complement the range of needs that Maslow conveniently outlined for us in his hierarchy.

If you are Harvard, you may differentiate yourself by being highly ranked or historically first. If you are Berkeley, you may differentiate yourself by being publicly funded or by being a bit edgy and quirky. If you are Westmont in Santa Barbara, you may differentiate yourself by upholding Christian values or by being ideally perched between the ocean and mountains.

"The driving philosophy behind differentiation is the belief

Plumber A
always arrives looking great

Plumber B
always arrives and
finishes on time

Plumber C
offers the lowest price

Differentiation contributes to brand expectation.
How are *you* differentiated from your competitors?

_____

_____

_____

_____

that customers don't buy sameness," writes former Coca-Cola®
CMO Sergio Zyman. "Differentiation is what separates you from
the pack."[3] But differentiation is not the brand. Even announcing
or broadcasting that choice to differentiate (i.e., departure from
expectation) is not the brand. The plumbers in our example above
aren't determining the brand. The consumers are determining the
brand, based on consistent delivery of the differentiating factor.
Your consumers define how well you are delivering on what you say
you are.

Of course, you *can* influence what people think. You *can* consistently deliver what you say you will to help strengthen your brand.
And you *can* supply information to support your claims. Indeed,
each of the schools mentioned above produces engaging websites,
beautifully printed viewbooks, compelling emails and letters to
describe their greatest assets to separate themselves from their
competitors. But these communication tools are not their brands.
Their brands are determined by users (current students, faculty and
staff), prospective students and their families, alumni, and high
school counselors. Further, their brands are determined by professional colleagues at other institutions, who annually cast their
ballots for the *U.S. News &World Report* rankings. Their brands are
determined by the encounters that these constituents—and many
others—have with these institutions on a daily, evolving basis.

....

So to recap: consumers control your brand, based on their expectations of and experiences with you.

Today, we can take that observation one step further and say that, due to the Internet, consumers control your brand even more, because they have access to more information—*and to each other*.

In the olden days—before 1998—the public didn't have as much access to information. The public was dependent on what they heard or read in the press. They were influenced by what they saw on television, heard on the radio, and read in magazines and on 48-foot outdoor signs. Since their access to information was limited, it was easier to control what the public saw. Corporations and institutions hired advertisers and marketers to tell the public what they wanted them to hear. Sure, people could talk to one another—"word of mouth" is nothing new, after all—but they had to meet at the market or church, or visit a neighbor or call a friend. And those "old-fashioned" communication efforts took time and imposition. Social circles were smaller. With few exceptions, one person's influence was significantly limited. So it was easy for marketers to think that they "controlled" their brands. Advertising, at that time, was clearly a more powerful medium.

Now, however, the Internet has flattened the processes of marketing exchange. By gaining access to information and direct links to products and services, consumers' sense of power and entitlement skyrocketed. The need for retailers and "middlemen" substantially declined. And, as consumer power escalated, consumer trust plummeted. Most "secrets" disappeared. We can know the inner workings of corporations. We can capture information to make important choices. We can easily discover opportunities. We can also find failures or misdeeds. Further, the speed of access to this information changed our behaviors. We can know the instant a sale begins at the Gap® or Gilt® and place an immediate order.

Access to the Internet allowed everyone on board to contribute, making *everyone* on both sides of the exchange equation equal participants. Certainly sellers of goods and services had a new avenue to consumers. And this access was direct and personalized; this exceptional medium made one-to-one marketing possible. This was a seller's dream: direct and fairly unhindered access to one buyer. The flipside was that buyers had direct access to sellers *and* buyers— and to all their family and friends. This direct access, in short time, displaced and devalued the seller as the transaction- and opinion-leader, and transferred power to the consumer. After all, whom are you going to believe? Your Aunt Sally and your best friend? Or the owners of Pottery Barn®? Someone you know personally and trust? Or someone who really just wants you to buy stuff?

So today, at best, you may be able to manage a brand. Controlling your brand is likely out of the question. And traditional "branding" tactics are out of step with the times. Kevin Roberts, CEO of Saatchi and Saatchi, in his book *Lovemarks*,[4] declares, "Brands have run out of juice." Indeed they have.

But there is an alternative that is right on for right now.

---

1 Neumeier, Marty. *The Brand Gap*. Berkeley: New Riders Publishing, 2003.

2 Ries, Al, and Jack Trout. *Positioning: The Battle for Your Mind*. New York: McGraw-Hill, 1981.

3 Zyman, Sergio, and Armin Brott. *The End of Advertising as We Know It*. New Jersey: John Wiley & Sons, Inc., 2002.

4 Roberts, Kevin. *Lovemarks: The Future Beyond Brands*. New York: powerHouse Books, 2005.

CHAPTER 3:

Beyond Branding: Coherence®

In the advertising class I teach at the University of Notre Dame, I bring a candy bar for each student on a certain day. As you can clearly tell by that, I am a very good teacher.

On the appointed day, I make sure that every student has a different candy bar brand, all the way down to Zagnut® and Zero®. I am usually rewarded for this by grins. I remove a crisp, five-dollar bill from my wallet. (When I began teaching years ago, I used to pull out a single dollar, but today's students are far more demanding; they won't play along for anything under five bucks.) I hold the bill up in the air and say to my students, "Let's market." After a silent moment or two, a bold student will shout, "I have M & Ms®. I'll sell them for five bucks."

Not to be outdone, other students join in, calling out the names of their candy bars.

I shake my head at each offer, but provide no other information. The students begin to think a little harder. They start to offer more. "This Hershey's® bar is king size," one might say. Or, "This KitKat® has several bars. You can have them all for five bucks."

Still nothing from me. They grow confused, then a little frustrated. Finally, one of the students will ask—often just rhetorically—the million-dollar question. "Well, what DO you want?"

"Aha!" I say. "How can you find out?" A light goes on in the faces of these future ad men and women. From here, the class can take one of any number of forms. Sometimes they create a survey for me. Sometimes they open up an informal discussion. Sometimes they try to figure out my preferences based on what they already know about me. But eventually, they determine that I prefer almonds to peanuts, milk chocolate to dark, and that I have a soft spot for coconut.

After that, the kid who has the Almond Joy® knows all she has to do is put it in my hand, and the five-dollar bill is hers. Instead of shouting out features and benefits or continually sweetening the pot, she can make the sale without saying a word.

That's coherence.

Let me explain.

...

At its most basic level, Phillip Kotler tells us, marketing is exchange.[1] Two parties each have something they want to provide

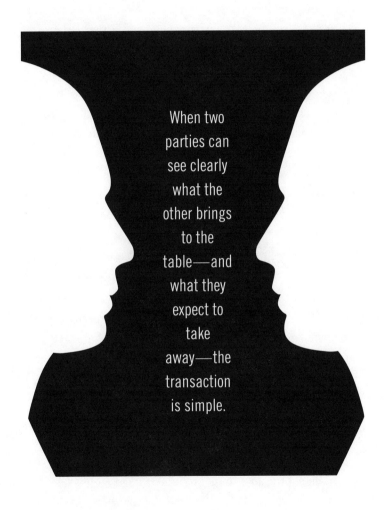

When two parties can see clearly what the other brings to the table—and what they expect to take away—the transaction is simple.

and something they hope to receive. When both parties can see clearly what the other brings to the table, and what they expect to take away—when there is coherence between the two parties—the transaction is simple.

Unfortunately, parties to an exchange do not often find such clarity. Coherence demands a high level of shared understanding. The unit of currency, the standards for quality, and even the vocabulary have to be the same. Both parties must cohere to—and "co-hear"—the same messages about what is being supplied and what is being demanded. If I had just said I liked nuts in my candy bar, instead of specifically mentioning my love of almonds and coconut, the guy who held the Mr. Goodbar® no doubt would have come forward. But that would not have been my meaning, and no matter how he argued his case, he wouldn't have been able to make a sale. A lack of specificity would keep us from coherence.

It's apparent achieving coherence is no small task. It dwarfs, or more correctly, encompasses, branding. Does that mean managing your branding isn't a good investment? Of course it doesn't mean that. Promoting your brand is still a relatively easy and powerful way to increase your market appeal. Brands are still alive and well. Megabrands and powerfully appreciated products and services—or as Kevin Roberts suggests, "lovemarks"—still exist. Yet the times require that you must be very clear about your brand.

Taking a coherence perspective on marketing means, however, that we should consider "branding" the tail and not the dog. And while we at RHB/The Agency are on the forefront of coherence marketing, we are by no means the only ones noticing that branding is just the tip of a massive marketing iceberg. "We have moved away from the time in which advertising's main function was to create awareness and favorable attitudes for a product," writes Daniel Morel, chairman and CEO of Wunderman. "We are smack in the middle of an era in which the focus is on the customer's experiences with the brand and his or her subsequent behavior."

In other words, a brand is likely one part of a shared under-standing of an exchange. While it is critical to know your brand "inside out," we would argue that it is now even more important to know your brand "outside in." At the same time that you have full knowledge of your integrated marketing efforts, you need to also understand your brand from the viewpoint of capricious consumers, given their broad and immediate access to information about you.

Lois Kelly, a partner at Beeline Labs and a former senior vice president at one of the largest PR firms in the world, underscores this notion of two-way exchange between marketers and customers:

> *"Marketing's purpose is to involve customers, helping them to understand the value of an organization or product to their wants and needs. [...] Like great teaching, the goal of marketing is not to assert conclusions but to engage an audience in a dialogue, which leads people to discoveries on their own."* [2]

...

From what these marketers have said, and from my classroom exercise with the candy bars, you're probably recognizing that research plays a key role in developing coherence. That's true.

(So true, in fact, that I'm going to return to several of these ideas in subsequent chapters.) But the kind of research that leads to coherence isn't always a simple matter. All too often, market research aims solely to discover what consumers want, in a very narrow sense. That may be fine if you are just hawking a candy bar, and your candy bar is at least a little different from everyone else's. But if you are hoping to sell consumers on something much more complex, enduring and life-changing—say, a college education, for example—you want to know much more. You want to know what your prospective customers expect, and even where those expectations came from. You want to know what misconceptions they have about what a college experience is all about, and which of those misconceptions can be changed. When your customers are teens, you want to know which of their tastes and likings are developmental and which are generational. You want to know who influences them and how—and if they even realize it. You have to know where your prospective customer is coming from. Even more important, you have to know where she hopes to go. You have to know how she imagines her life will change once she has bought what you or your competition is selling.

It's heady stuff. And believe it or not, it's only one side of the market research equation. That's because you don't want to limit your research to finding out about your customers. You also want to research ways of allowing customers to find out about you and what you bring to the market. To do that, you have to know who you really are (another idea I'll return to shortly). But I'll even go one step further. You have to be willing to consider change, too.

Let me explain. Remember that old chestnut of a marketing model we all studied in college, the 4 Ps?[3] They were Product, Place, Promotion and Price; and we were told that successful marketing is a workable mix of all four. (Today, some marketers teach up to seven Ps, adding packaging, positioning and people.)

Well, everything old is new again, because you can consider the 4 Ps an outline (albeit a rather skeletal one) for the kind of self-research you ought to consider as a part of your marketing efforts. Too often, we let marketing efforts focus exclusively on the Promotion aspect of the Ps, but if I had to single one out as most important, it's Product. You need to take an unflinching look at your product as an absolute prerequisite to a coherent exchange. If your customer wants a peanut butter Twix®, he's not going to be fooled by the caramel version you're offering. And if it turns out all your customers share his preference, you better consider changing the recipe, and quick. You can still love what you sell, and see its special merits and distinctions. But you can sell it more easily and successfully if you've explored those qualities in a deeper context and been willing to question your own presuppositions and dearly held beliefs about your product.

The other three Ps are important, too, and it bears a moment of explanation to describe how a marketing model developed for widgets can translate to higher education (or other intangibles).

In any economy, but especially the current one, it's easy to see how the P of Price is related. It's possible to lose access to a key segment of your prospective customers by pricing them out of the market. It's also possible to under-price what you are offering. The role of tuition discounting alone could merit (no pun intended) an entire dissertation exploring how it affects student recruitment. Many of the factors at play may be unique to your situation, and certainly a volatile market and dwindling capital bases complicate the issue even further. My point here is not to encourage you to take a particular stance on pricing matters. Rather, I want to emphasize pricing's central role in marketing and its interrelationships with the other factors at play.

Place, the third P, may mean deciding on a tabletop display versus an endcap, if you're in the widget business. But what does it mean in higher education? Think more broadly about how you reach your would-be market, not with your message, but with your actual product. Some obvious "delivery" considerations—should you offer evening courses, or an online degree program?—may come to mind. But delve a little more deeply into the issue of how an even wider segment of students could have access to your programs, and you may start thinking along even more profound lines. Do you need a different mix of majors? Are you serving the needs of Latino teens? Is your mission too exclusive? Are you competing for the right students? Are you competing with the *right schools*? Think of the Place P as the one that explores access in all its forms, the one that places your education within reach of ever-better constituencies.

Once you have learned all you can about your customer *and* have explored the other three Ps (Product, Place and Price), you can begin to look at the P of Promotion with the information you need to be effective. A common misperception is that promotion *is* marketing. But while it may be the most visible aspect of

The 4 Ps form an outline for important questions you should ask yourself.
How would you describe your institution using this outline?

_____   _____
_____   _____
_____   _____
_____   _____

PROMOTION   PRODUCT

PLACE   PRICE

_____   _____
_____   _____
_____   _____
_____   _____

marketing, without minding the other Ps, promotion is empty or even wasteful. And only when you have all four Ps together does coherence become possible.

...

Let me give a practical example in Warner Pacific College. As I mentioned in Chapter 1, among Warner Pacific's many assets is its location in central Portland, Oregon. The campus is a short bicycle ride from the popular, urban Hawthorne District. Its neighborhood is one of the most diverse in the Northwest; you'll likely hear as many as 17 or 18 different languages being spoken within a small radius of the College. And the campus is within two walking blocks of an area marked for substantial crime. Now, some would say that Warner Pacific's location isn't an asset; it's a liability. But that's not a perspective shared by the College's leadership. Look at how they've used the four Ps to advantage in this singular characteristic of their location.

PRODUCT: Given the resources of its location and the high interest in urban ministry within the College's market, Warner Pacific initiated a program in Urban Studies. By playing to a given strength, and unafraid of change, the College opened new windows of opportunity to a specialized national market, using its campus and Portland as an outstanding learning laboratory.

PRICE: In response to a renewed interest in serving the market closest to home, and to be true to its mission of "providing students from diverse backgrounds an education that prepares them for the spiritual, moral, social, vocational and technological challenges of the 21st century," the College, in 2008, actually reduced tuition by 23 percent to make a Warner Pacific education more accessible to more families. In fact, the new price point was 37 percent less than the average tuition of other private institutions in Washington and Oregon. By reconfiguring its pricing strategy, the College was able to broaden its reach to more students, an appropriate choice given its potential market.

PLACE: To make the front campus more inviting to those in the neighborhood, a retrofitting of the student center improved both internal morale and external perception. With an art gallery, an open cafeteria, community meeting rooms, and—oh yeah! a more accessible admission office—the new facility makes a powerful first impression. The College also extended its reach to include degree programs for working adults, both on its primary campus and at a convenient, freeway-accessible, satellite facility less than two miles from the main campus. More recently, Warner Pacific has expanded to four additional sites.

PROMOTION: Warner Pacific launched a significant brand-awareness campaign that included a new visual identity and new print and online promotional materials. But more important, the College created new annual events that welcome the entire community to campus. In addition, the College plans recurring service-day events that include students, faculty and staff in community-improvement endeavors, the most popular of which involved sprucing up the dog-friendly park area around Mount Tabor, right in the College's backyard. Now, families with children frequently visit the park with pets and friends, encountering the campus on a regular basis.

Of course, Warner Pacific invested and engaged in dozens of other carefully considered decisions to ensure its coherence. But in this aspect of location alone, Warner Pacific demonstrated a willingness to match experience with perception.

And that is the heart of coherence.

...

---

1 "A Generic Concept of Marketing," Journal of Marketing (1972), Vol. 36, Number 2, pp. 46-54

2 Kelly, Lois. *Beyond Buzz*. New York: AMACOM, 2007.

3 My thanks to Woody Self who used Jerome McCarthy's *Basic Marketing (Irwin, 1960)* as a text while I was at Spring Arbor. My 1981 edition still sits on my shelf as reference. And to Norman Bell and Harry McKinney at Michigan State who connected the dots related to the 4Ps, each in his own way.

CHAPTER 4

The eBay Example: Some Keys to Coherence

Without a doubt, eBay offers one of the best, if not the most copious, examples of coherence in marketing today. On eBay, you can watch coherence in action, firsthand, thousands of times a day. Here are sellers, offering items from the ridiculous to the sublime, nearly perfectly aligned with buyers seeking same. A rare first edition of Hemingway. A Flying Nun lunchbox. A Tiffany lampshade. A 1950s Elvis poster. White elephants. Whatnots. Almost everything under the sun. And somewhere, someday, maybe today, buyers for all of it. As coherent as can be.

What makes eBay work? What makes its buyers and sellers cohere? Several factors:

1. Respect for a discerning consumer

One of the primary factors underlying eBay's high level of marketing coherence is an assumption that buyers are intelligent people who know what they want. The eBay ethos is to describe a product honestly, then stand back and let the buyers decide if they want it, and how badly. (Sort of reminds you of parents who "peddle" their children to admissions officers, doesn't it?) While consumers may need additional information, or even education, the notion of "false consciousness" that consumers may be deluded about what they want simply doesn't apply on eBay.

The issue of what a consumer can or cannot be assumed to know definitely looms large in higher education, particularly in recruitment marketing. It's commonplace to hear that "kids don't know what's good for them, or even what they want from a college education." And the very premise of education is that those who know are teaching those who don't know. Yet it is dangerous to assume your audiences are wholly informed.

Far be it from me to suggest that seventeen-year-olds (or even their parents) are truly sophisticated and savvy consumers of college educations. And certainly, college is a complex, complicated subject to have to promote. But, while I believe that college representatives do have a role to play in educating prospective students about higher ed choices, I don't think this education should take place at the cost of a thorough understanding of and appreciation for those consumers' goals, interests, aspirations, core beliefs and values. A little respect, or a lot, is always in order.

The University of South Florida, for instance, struck an ideal balance between "educating" and "respecting" its prospective student markets—particularly as it sought to improve its academic profile and retention rate by recruiting best-fit students from the very beginning. For starters, the admissions office developed a tool for high-school guidance counselors: an "initial eligibility grid" that charts the minimum high school GPAs and standardized test scores used by the University in evaluating first-year applicants. In essence, this information was developed to be completely transparent about the kind of student most likely to succeed in the educational environment found at USF so that counselors could help steer "discerning consumers" toward or away from the University as appropriate. Furthermore, USF chose to place this grid online, where it can be accessed not only by counselors, but also by anyone who wishes to see and use it.

Complementing this tool were many others that moved away from communicating that "USF *is* for everyone" and toward specifying whom the University *is* for: a brochure that highlights the University's dynamic Honors Program; ads that translate the benefits of being a "top 50 research university" into 16-year-old-appropriate messages about "exploration" and "discovery"; a viewbook that enthusiastically embraces the institution's size and location, emphasizing the energy, diversity and opportunity that are attendant with larger, more cosmopolitan campuses and cities. The purpose of such specificity and clarity? To equip and allow audiences to make their own, reasoned, discerning judgments as to how well USF fits with their particular abilities, interests and ambitions—in short, to demonstrate respect for the University's partners in exchange.

2. Accountability

eBay also works because it's a pretty solidly accountable system. Of all the checks and balances in place to ensure that buyers and sellers meet each other's expectations, none is more powerful than the rating system eBay uses. Fail to mention that missing piece in your vintage Clue game, and earn yourself a dismal evaluation from your buyer. Send a late payment for your newest treasure, and your seller will pan you, too. Then, ever after, anyone on eBay can check your rating and decide if you're the kind of party with whom they wish to do business.

Not long ago, we worked with an institution whose administration identified the school as a brand leader in career-focused education. Yet, as we interviewed students and faculty, we discovered that few of the institution's limited programs offered internship opportunities. We also noticed that the career office was closeted in a small hideaway—and the position of placement director seemed like a revolving door. Corporate recruiters rarely came to campus, we learned; and as we extended our research to alumni, few credited the school with helping them succeed in a profession. Of course, those findings don't align with a "career-focused education" brand, and with social media increasingly interconnecting students and parents, the institution was on a collision course with accountability. Change was definitely in order.

Now, before you start casting stones, think about your claim to "personal attention" or "close student-faculty interaction" or "leadership development." Do you really deliver on that claim to differentiation? What would indicate that to be true? You can think of enrollment, retention and giving rates as a rough equivalent to eBay's accountability system. Your audiences may not always use a five-star scale (though on some web sites, they actually will), but they *will* be holding you accountable.

3. Frankness

Related to respect and accountability is frankness. Honesty to the point of bluntness is definitely the norm on eBay. If you don't believe me, do a search on the word "chipped," "bent," "broken" or "damaged." You'll spend all day reading the descriptions that contain these words. But even through the frankness, the listings build excitement for their products. After all, if you've waited your whole life for that last Scooby-Doo drinking glass to round out your collection, maybe you don't care if Shaggy's shirt is faded. And if you do, best to find out now, before your expectations of Shaggy perfection are dashed.

Consider the steps that the University of Georgia took to more honestly engage the African-American community in its recruitment efforts. UGA began with research focusing on its primary market, asking current students and faculty to assess the "user experience." Though some of the feedback wasn't particularly pleasant to hear (it was, in fact, painful), administrators at UGA were intent on improving the quality of their product and the truthfulness of their promotional materials. Committed efforts in academic and co-curricular programming yielded progress on UGA deliverables. And a bold move in the admissions office helped with messaging.

UGA's new recruitment campaign was built on the theme "From

Here On Out"—a phrase that conveys the thrilling possibility inherent in strong research and international study programs, but at the same time communicates the University's renewed commitments to doing things a bit differently. Further, rather than creating a multicultural brochure targeted only to African-Americans, the admissions team created a mailing for *every* prospective student: a piece that opened by truthfully detailing how UGA was late to the game in welcoming African-American students into its gates.

The piece went on to detail, however, the ways in which the institution has changed—and improved—since that time, describing how the University has been enriched by encouraging diversity in all its many forms. And across the center of the piece, in a bold, banner headline, ran the unequivocal message, "Our community is stronger with the voices of many." This important language was soon adopted campus-wide, appearing on computer screensavers, giveaway tote bags and orientation t-shirts. And ultimately, this commitment to coherence—to telling the truth—influenced real change at UGA, including a significant jump in African-American student enrollment.

...

There may be many more reasons for the highly coherent exchange that takes place on eBay, but respect, accountability and frankness are among the most significant for marketing in general. And while the specifics of how these factors play out in e-commerce may not transfer perfectly to our higher ed worlds, most of us can take some lessons here. A nailed-down, well-articulated brand can't help you if you are deficient, dishonest, disrespectful or unaccountable for your end of a bargain. In fact, in those cases, a brand can even work against you, since a reputation for poor quality, poor communication or poor reliability can become a part of a brand, just as positive characteristics can.

Think of "integrity" as the core value for "coherence" in marketing. It's an appropriate word in two senses. First, in its less common and broader meaning, "integrity" denotes "wholeness." And coherence demands this as well. It requires us to look at the entire picture of our exchange with others, not just the moment of sale, and certainly not just the promotional side of the transaction.

The second and more common meaning of integrity—"a sense of rectitude or ethics"—is also pertinent to the concept of marketing coherence we've put forward here. Central to what we've been discussing are several important commitments: to present our interests as "sellers" honestly, to respect our customers, and to seek a fair exchange for both parties. Far from complicating market transactions, these commitments will reduce them to their simplest and truest form, and they will empower you to connect with your consumers at a level of engagement that goes well beyond a brand.

CHAPTER 5

(With) Whom Do You Need to Cohere (Co-Hear)?

For the students in my advertising class trying to sell me a candy bar (see Chapter 3), this question is a no-brainer. After all, there's only one guy in the room who's waving around a five-dollar bill and professing a sugar craving.

But in a world as complex and multi-faceted as higher ed, the answer may not be as clear-cut; and without a pretty thorough understanding of how your particular institution does (or should) respond to this question, your marketing endeavors don't stand a chance. So before we commence with some specifics on how to arrive at coherence, let's take a moment to identify—and prioritize—the audiences who will be critical to your success.

Peter Drucker, in his thought-provoking essays captured in *The Five Most Important Questions You Will Ever Ask About Your Nonprofit Organization*[1], smartly suggests that you begin by focusing on your *primary* audience. For schools, that would be students and their surrounding support network of faculty and staff.

"Wait, wait, wait," I can hear you saying. "What about donors? And legislators? And boards? And parents! Those are pretty primary to *us*, anyway." Of course they are important, and we'll get to them in just a bit. But they are not your primary audience. Your primary audience consists of those for whom your mission is written. A college would simply not exist for any reasonable purpose were it not for students.

Here's a way to think of your primary audience. Picture a Callaway® HX Hot Plus® golf ball. You've got one lying around the house, right? Constructed for improved distance, this beauty is made of three parts: It has a Polybutadiene core (that's hard rubber to you golf-ball novices) that is wrapped in a speed layer of DuPont™ HPF, which is then wrapped in an outer, harder shell of Ionomer with HEX Aerodynamics. Have that pictured, do you? Great, because that's a perfect image to illustrate your primary audience.

We noted before that your primary customer is the group your mission is written to serve. At a college or university, remember, that would be currently enrolled students in any size or shape they come. Residential 18-year-olds. Forty-something working adults. Online. Offline. Inline. All currently enrolled students. Not prospective students. Not former students (alumni). *Current students.*

In our golf ball analogy, that amazing Polybutadiene core represents current students. Powerful stuff, that Polybutadiene—as are your students. They're powerful because they represent the audience you must satisfy most. They must be served well. They must benefit most from your mission. For them, you absolutely must deliver on your promises. If your mission is to create world leaders, then there will be future presidents, senators, CEOs and emperors among them, and you will have to offer services and programs to prepare them. If you exist to equip students for careers, then your career-planning officers will be top-notch professionals; corporate recruiters will be storming your campus to retain new hires; and your students will be launching careers immediately after graduation. If you are educating pastors and missionaries, your students will expect preparation second-to-none for filling pulpits and engaging diverse cultures and places. If you are all about delivering a clear foundation in the liberal arts, your humanities core has to rock.

In other words, you have to meet—or better yet, exceed—the expectations of your primary audience. If you do not make the user-experience on a par with—or better than—your claims, you should sell your campus right now, or merge with another school that is serious about doing so. On today's golf course of higher ed, amateurs won't be long-term players. The competition is too great, the cost is too high and the market is too savvy.

Not long ago, while on site at Post University, a for-profit residential liberal arts college in Connecticut whose institutional tagline includes the phrase "student-focused," we were taking a campus tour with Marcelo, the director of marketing. When we walked into the dining commons, he bumped into a student who was helping with one of his projects on campus. Marcelo took the occasion to ask the student how things were going and if there was anything she could think of that would make her experience better. "Well, I'm pretty happy with things as they are," she said. "But it would be great if we could have an occasional shuttle van scheduled for trips into town." "Done!" was Marcelo's response. Clearly, he understood his primary market—and the importance of delivering what you say you will deliver. And, indeed, today a designated regular shuttle service transports Post students to destinations throughout town.

(Someone—or everyone—reading this right now is saying, "That's just giving in to those spoiled Gen Y brats." But remember that those precious treasures of Boomer and Gen X parents are the customers for whom you exist. And here's another alert: Neil Howe, the expert on generational studies and the author of *Millennials Rising,* predicts that Gen X moms and dads will not be helicopter parents, but rather stealth bombers in that they sneak in with hard-hitting demands. Duck and cover, baby.)[2]

...

So current students represent the heart of your primary audience; they're that all-important inner core in our three-layered golf ball. But let's extend this metaphor further.

According to DuPont's website, wrapped around that core in the Callaway HX Hot Plus, you'll find a layer of HPF resins that "offer a breakthrough combination of resilience, softness and toughness" to help drive the ball farther. In our illustration, this resin wrapper is your teaching faculty. These distinguished women and men, like the resin, equip your students to go the distance. They must be resilient, given the demands of their students, and they must offer gentle guidance and "tough love" to set a proper course for their protégés.

Your faculty is also part of your primary customer group. And, as you well know, they have their own set of needs, about which they can be rather vocal. Listen to those needs—even the outrageous ones—and, to the extent that you are able, meet them; because professors are inextricably linked to your students and, though the mission isn't directly about them, they are part of your product. What's more, they're essential ambassadors in recruitment. The University of South Florida acknowledges the power of faculty in convincing admitted students to enroll. USF developed a "BFF (Best Friends Forever)" communications strategy that engages faculty and staff from academic departments and programs in personal contacts with their most promising and qualified admitted students.

And what about that protective outer layer of our Callaway golf ball? The tough stuff? You guessed it: staff and administration. Presidents and senior officers who set the course and manage. Directors and coordinators who carry out the plans. Directors of admission. Deans of Student Life. Athletic directors. Controllers. Chaplains. The people on your campus who hold it all together, getting hit hard and often, and sheltering the students and faculty from the blows. And of course, the really thick-skinned and tough-shelled: cafeteria staff, admissions road warriors, data entry personnel, physical plant specialists. All of these significant members of the community are part of your primary audience. As employees, their needs must be met, too.

Collectively, your primary customer audience is the frontline of your marketing effort. So you should be asking, openly and often: What does your primary audience think about you? What are their needs? What's on their wish list? What would make their experiences with you better? Do you really know? If not, you'd better find out, stat. Because more public relations progress, recruitment success and capital campaign achievement rests in the hands—and especially on the lips—of your primary customers than any other audience you consider important.

Here again is that definition of coherence from an earlier chapter: Coherence is the discipline of ensuring a transparent connection between customer expectation (brand) and authentic user experience. Coherence is aligning what we deliver with what we say we deliver. Coherence engages customers in shaping a meaningful experience that meets their needs.

Make sure your efforts toward coherence focus first on your primary customer audience. Meet their needs. Exceed their expectations. Make raving fans. Because as we noted earlier, in a world defined by proliferating social media, you can be assured that your internal audiences are very closely connected to your external audiences.

Get it right with your primary customers, and you'll get it right.

...

Now, back to all those other people you were so insistent we not ignore: alumni, donors, parents, boards and a multitude of others.

When we begin working with new clients, we often prepare a chart of their various constituent audiences. In no time, given the plethora of "mouths to feed," the chart turns into a spidery web of primary, secondary and tertiary audiences. Our intent in preparing these charts is to help clarify our clients' marketing and communications efforts. But without fail, every time we flash that chart on the screen in our Keynote presentation, we hear an audible gasp, and someone (usually the communications director) declares, "No wonder I'm so exhausted!" Facing the reality of the breadth of your audiences indeed prompts mind-numbing thoughts on the enormous tasks of marketing. But we'll try to simplify things a bit here.

Let's return to the golf ball that represents your primary customers: the user-groups of students, faculty and staff. Say we're out on the links and you hit that Callaway golf ball supremely. I mean, you just walloped it. You really sent that ball sailing. In fact, let's say you hit that ball so hard, it jetted to outer space and is now out there spinning among the planets and stars. And like the sun, it's become the center of its own universe. (I am not talking about your favorite Millennial here, I'm talking about your golf ball.)

Have that pictured? Good, because now I'm going to introduce other audiences that orbit around your central, primary audience. (You advancement officers can relax now. I promise I'll talk about donors here.) If you have paper and pencil handy, this would be a good moment to grab them, so that you can draw your own "audience orbit chart." Or mark the one on page 51. But first, let's start by simply naming some secondary audiences. Here's a beginning list to prompt your imagination:

- Governing boards and trustees
- Moms and dads (lawnmowers, helicopters, stealths and idle 727s); guardians
- Other family members, including siblings who may be future admission candidates
- Alumni from all class years, academic programs, social organizations and residential affiliations
- Donors and "friends" of your institution
- State and federal legislators
- Other gatekeepers, such as alumni boards and advisory groups
- Prospective students, including any new markets you wish to pursue (in your list, you will want to identify all those markets you now serve and intend to serve)
- Church bodies, such as denominational leadership, local congregations, parishes or dioceses
- Employers of graduates, current and future
- Neighbors, meaning those who live around your campus and those in your local community, including chambers of commerce and local government
- Peers from other institutions
- Media in all its forms and reach around the globe (that will probably be a long list for you)

Now here's an assignment. Place each of those secondary audiences in orbit around your primary audience (the golf ball), according to their size and relative importance to the operation and success of your institution. Some of these audiences will be larger than others by virtue of their mass. Alumni, for example, will likely be much larger than some other groups. But parents may be closer in orbit, given their influence on and attachments to their children—your current and prospective students.

Perhaps a few examples will help. Remember those four institutions we introduced in Chapter 1? Let's examine some considerations that might go into creating their audience orbit chart.

- At Sweet Briar, when we define prospective students, we're only talking about female students, and they are in very close proximity to the core, given the College's dependence upon tuition income. And alumnae play a very significant role in the life of Sweet Briar. We might categorize them by geography in order to engage them in groups, or we might organize them by graduation year, since Sweet Briar has a number of longstanding student-life traditions that are aligned by class. Or we might consider organizing them by social organizations, since "Tap Clubs" (special-interest student groups) readily link students according to co-curricular interest.

- At the University of South Florida, we'd naturally keep state legislators close to the core, given the volatility of budgets and higher-education policy in that state. Likewise, we'd stay close to our neighbors in Tampa, but at the same time, reach to new audiences, including those out of state, for additional prospective students. And as an emerging institution, USF might place peer groups from other universities relatively close to the core, since they influence public perceptions about quality.

- UGA has a huge number of fiercely loyal alumni who are inextricably bound to the University, especially as athletic boosters of the "Bulldog nation"; this very large group might be closer to the core than at other institutions. In addition to state government, the UGA Foundations play an important role in posturing the fiscal capacity for the University, so those boards may also be close to the core.

- And at Warner Pacific College, the chart will include residents in the neighborhood, since local civic leaders will be essential in helping to advance campus-improvement plans. And the Church of God, which originally founded the College, will continue to have an important hand in shaping the direction for Warner Pacific, so it will appear close to the golf-ball core.

Obviously, the examples above illustrate only a few considerations that each of these institutions would make in building an audience orbit chart. And your specific circumstances will be very different from these.

In fact, no two audience orbiting charts will be the same. Seriously. Your audience profile might be linked to your geography. Your audience(s) might be differentiated by academic profiles or admittance qualifications. Yours could be religiously affiliated. Or connected by political or economic structures. Even if there are two

Who orbits around your primary audiences?

Fill in the circles with your audiences; add more circles and orbital rings as needed.

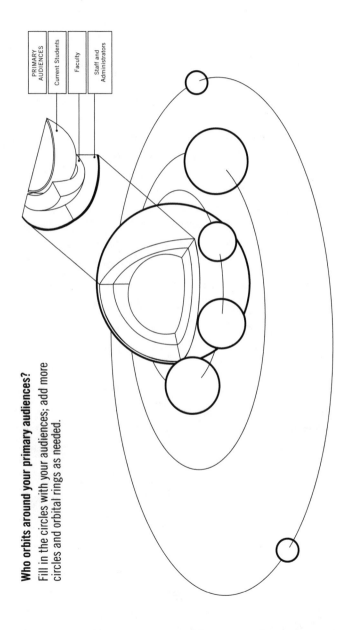

PRIMARY AUDIENCES

Current Students

Faculty

Staff and Administrators

private colleges in the same town, it's unlikely they share the exact same audience chart. If nothing else, their alumni audiences differ. If you are one of ten public universities in your state, none of you shares quite the same audiences orbiting about you in the same way. Naturally, you'll find overlap, but the sum total of your audience orbit is wholly distinctive. And that may be what distinguishes you from all others. It may be, in fact, what keeps you alive.

But hear me on this: Do not confuse your unique audience set with an automatic capacity to survive as you are right now. Just look at the news. Some schools aren't making it, and others will be out of the running within the year. Read about Cascade College, Vennard College, College of Sante Fe or Taylor University Fort Wayne. Each had distinctive missions and audiences, yet none had sufficient breadth or depth of audience to realistically stake a sustainable claim in the marketplace. All may be fine schools with noble causes, yet none carried sufficient market size to keep them afloat.

That's why you have to work at coherence, ensuring that your deliverables match the needs of a sufficiently large customer base (or more likely, customer bases), and that you deliver—consistently and reliably—on your promises to *all* the audiences in your orbit.

---

1 Drucker, Peter. *The Five Most Important Questions.* San Francisco: Jossey-Bass, 2008.

2 Strauss, William, and Howe, Neil. *Millennials Go to College: Strategies for a New Generation on Campus.* American Association of College Registrars, 2003.

CHAPTER 6

En Route to Coherence: Locating Your Institution on the Marketing Map

Several years ago, business took me to downtown Boston, which at that time was in the throes of the "Big Dig," the city's enormous roadway and tunneling infrastructure project. A colleague and I had flown in late in the evening and had a client meeting the next morning. The weather was poor, and I was glad that our Hertz rental car was equipped with a global positioning system. As annoying as the system's mechanized voice could be ("Right turn in point five miles"), Randy and I appreciated the clear direction as we left the hotel and made our way through the maze of streets and highways under construction.

Near Faneuil Hall, however, in the middle of a critical voice instruction, the system cut out. I looked at the small screen, hoping that the bright pink arrows would guide me when the voice did not. Instead, I saw a green band running left to right across the screen with a text message indicating that the system was "seeking third satellite." While Randy scavenged for the complimentary city map from Hertz, we started a conversation about GPS programming.

Global positioning systems may rely on space-age technology—satellites—but they also employ an age-old methodology to guide befuddled travelers like Randy and me. That methodology is called "navigational triangulation," and reduced to its basics, it is simply a matter of using the intersection of lines from three points to locate someone or something in space. Before there were satellites, someone seeking to pinpoint a location could use three landmarks to achieve the same results—though he or she wouldn't have the luxury of a car that offers audible step-by-step directions.

As Randy and I reviewed our collective knowledge of GPS and triangulation, we were struck—not by another car, I am happy to report—but by an analogy. As we creative types are prone to do, Randy and I started to connect the dots between the idea of navigational triangulation and our work as marketing communicators for our clients in the not-for-profit sector. We observed that, like a GPS, today's organizations and institutions need three perspectives in order to position themselves accurately within their environments. The "satellites" our clients must seek are:

- *Who they are.* Beyond what their official mission and values statements say, today's not-for-profits—colleges and universities, especially—need to know what effect they really have on the world around them, and why;

- *What messages they are currently communicating about themselves.* Institutions must understand not only what is intended, but also what is implied or suggested by the look, feel, image and content of their marketing efforts;

- *What external audiences understand and believe about the organization.* What consumers say you are—regardless of whether those perceptions are accurate in your eyes—defines your "brand."

These three "satellites" help colleges and universities—and other not-for-profit organizations—define their places in the market. They can identify your true points of differentiation and meaning, and in a very real sense, locate your organization on the landscape of competing groups and messages. Quite simply, these three satellites will put your institution on the map.[1]

It must be said, however: you cannot hobble along guided by only one or two of these satellites. It simply won't work. Just as Randy and I were left lost and scrambling when one of our satellite signals was interrupted, you cannot pinpoint your one-and-only market position without the aid of all three of these perspectives. And without knowing that position, you cannot move toward coherence.

Here's a good example of the three satellites in action. As I mentioned in Chapter 1, at a critical moment in the history of Sweet Briar College, RHB was invited to assist in developing messaging to support recruitment efforts. You may recall this first-tier, single-gender institution was threatened by declining enrollments. We began our work by seeking the "first satellite" perspective *(who are we?*) through market research on campus. (At RHB, we employ a signature research methodology called *Circles of Influence*[SM], a variation of the traditional focus group that allows us to explore the relationships and experiences that characterize life on a particular campus.) During our *Circles* conversations, we consistently heard students, faculty and staff refer to the students as "girls" rather than "women." We were interested in this use of language that, at first blush, seemed less than politically correct. Yet, at Sweet Briar, the use of "girls" was perfectly acceptable.

Another interesting observation that arose from our "first satellite" investigation: In almost every one of our interviews, someone would whisper as an aside that the school's colors were pink and green. After a few days of repeatedly hearing this, we began to ask questions about the apparent reluctance to publicly discuss school colors. We were informed that the issue was a campus sore spot, because some members in the community considered those colors "too girly."

Lastly, our conversations on campus introduced us to an array of beautiful, if a little quirky, annual traditions and activities that connected the community in meaningful and lasting ways. We were told of the custom of passing along graduation gowns from one class to the next, each year adding a memento from the graduate; of tap clubs, the Sweet Briar social organizations structured around extracurricular interests; of class rings and personalized mugs; of annual Founder's Day processions. Of course, we heard scores of other interesting messaging platforms, as well, but I'm calling attention to these particular findings to make a specific point.

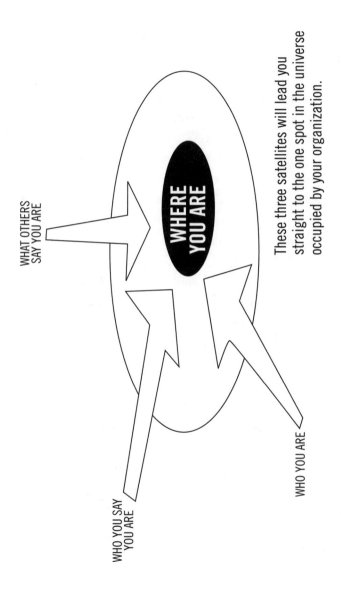

WHAT OTHERS SAY YOU ARE

WHO YOU ARE

WHO YOU SAY YOU ARE

WHERE YOU ARE

These three satellites will lead you straight to the one spot in the universe occupied by your organization.

When we moved to the "second satellite" portion *(what do we say about ourselves?)* of our study, examining the College's current marketing and communication efforts, we discovered that while the academic quality message seemed clearly conveyed, little attention was given to the interesting community experiences that characterize Sweet Briar. We also noticed that, at the time, all the College's marketing messages referred to students as "women," which we noticed in contrast to our conversations on campus. And the packaging of the College's marketing tools employed a palette of cool colors: blue, green and silver. (Again, I'm highlighting a few observations from the hundreds we considered.)

These findings helped formulate some questions that we were able to pose to external markets in our "third satellite" research *(what do others say we are?)*. Specifically, given the College's needs and goals at that time, we sought to understand the perceptions of prospective students, their mothers, and alumnae with various demographics targeted to specific geographic areas. Among other topics, we wanted to know how audiences perceived the use of the words "girl" and "woman." We wanted to know to what extent they valued tradition and memory-making experiences. We wanted to know the associations they made with the color pink.

With the insights gained from all three satellites, we found opportunity. We discovered a niche among academically qualified, engaged, confident, fun-loving 17-year-olds. We garnered courage and were emboldened. We uncovered a space that only Sweet Briar could occupy. As a result, Sweet Briar launched a risky, but remarkable, recruitment campaign in 2005, based on the theme

"Think is for Girls." The accompanying visuals implemented the school colors of pink and green, and—without diminishing the messages of academic quality—highlighted the closeness (and even the quirkiness of the traditions mentioned earlier) of the Sweet Briar community. As we noted, the campaign yielded positive results for the College. It's also garnered substantial attention from the higher ed community. But the campaign likely would not have taken off, had we relied on less than three satellites of perspective. Let me explain.

Had we only the results of the first satellite question *(who are we?)*, we may have dismissed the use of the word "girl" as too detached from the formality of higher ed, if not too uncharacteristic of education's commitments to political correctness. We may have overlooked the option of pink and green as a color scheme, given the tentativeness we heard in our interviews. (Remember, interview participants *whispered* this information.) From satellite two *(what do we say we are?)*, our reluctance to act on the language and color would likely have been confirmed, since the existing materials shied away from those topics and tones. The third satellite *(what do others say we are?)* gave us the open window to pursue new messaging and packaging, since employing "girl" language, a new color palette and revised messaging yielded positive response. Armed with all three perspectives, Sweet Briar took a bold move to the front of the line.

You can, too.

---

1 In his book *Truth, Lies and Advertising*, Jon Steel also makes a case for the application of the triangulation theory, suggesting that good advertising needs three perspectives: the agency's, the consumer's and the client's. And my friend, James Hillman, who, in addition to being a successful business owner, is also a pilot, says that, when flying, five perspectives are required for global positioning. He reminds me that since our marketing work is done on earth, however, three perspectives will suffice.

CHAPTER 7

Satellite One: Know Thyself

I am about to give away my age.

But I think it's important for you to know that I was influenced early by classical music and its vital messages: The Beatles. The Rolling Stones. Freddy and the Dreamers. And The Who.

This may explain why the first satellite question is so significant to me. And why I am an evangelist for answering the first satellite question before all others. Pete Townshend wrote some amazing lyrics that likely piqued my interest in probing the most critical question of all:

Who are you?

Who, who, who, who?

Who are you?

Who, who, who, who?

Are those lyrics inspired, or what? Perhaps we have Pete to thank for this book. (And if you are my age—or a loyalist of TV's *CSI*—you will now be humming this tune for weeks. Sorry about that.)

As anyone who has ever gone through adolescence knows, the road to self-awareness is fraught with pitfalls. And it doesn't get much easier in maturity. Even the most sincere and strenuous bursts of self-examination may come up short, revealing more of what we intend to be (or wish we were) than of what we actually are. A generation or so ago, as TQM and Stephen Covey's writings took hold in the business world, a mad dash began among organizations large and small to develop mission statements and enumerations of corporate values. These noble covenants presumably reflected the ideas and ideals that an organization already embodied—and perhaps, in some very abstract or qualified way, they did. But in our experience, statements of mission and values are far less reflections of day-to-day reality than they are formalized avowals of intent. They tell you as much about an organization as a couple's wedding ceremony tells you about the ins and outs of their marriage today.

Here's another problem with mission statements as organizational identities: Very often, these statements are so general as to be largely useless for the highly specific task of marketing. Sometimes they are even vacuous. This came home to me in force a year or two ago as I shopped in a small store that sells only batteries. A franchise of a national chain, the store proudly displayed the corporate mission statement on the wall. It read in part:

> "[Our]Mission Statement is to solve our customers' battery problems with availability, quality, service, and technical knowledge at an affordable price."

Boil off the buzzwords, and you get: "We sell batteries, and we try to be good at it." And in a battery store, too. Wonder of wonders.

Sarcasm aside, mission statements can be useful. They describe great causes. They can offer direction. They can be beautiful, even moving and inspiring. Most not-for-profits have missions that are far more important than selling batteries, and these missions are worthy of lofty language. Again, the analogy to wedding ceremonies is apt: the language of ceremony and promise plays an essential role that can be at the very heart of an organization (or a couple). But for neither newlyweds nor non-profits do ceremonial utterances offer a complete and detailed identity.

So if soul-searching won't tell you, how do you find out who you are? Ironically, the best way may be to ask someone else. For one thing, we get so accustomed to *us*, we fail to notice how special we are. I remember a few years ago, we had incorporated a symbol as a graphic element in some recruitment publications for one of our West Coast clients. The client asked me several times why we were using that symbol. I explained that it was the lovely image that appeared on their mosaic-laden chapel belltower, the most prominent building on their campus. Finally, during a phone call to review proofs, the client asked me, for the fourth or fifth time, about the origins of the symbol. In exasperation I said, "Please put down the phone, walk outside and look up. I'll wait on the line." Reluctantly, the client complied, and when he returned to the phone, I heard, "Well, I'll be! I've never noticed that before. It's beautiful." Sometimes, for whatever reason, we miss the beauty that is right under our noses—or over our heads. We've encountered institutions so transfixed on mimicking aspirational peers or parroting "best practices" that they lost sight of—and failed to celebrate—their own wonderful distinctiveness.

I also know that in higher ed, it's easy to become too chock full of how "special" we are. (No, no. Not you, of course. It's your colleagues and competitors who have the super-sized egos.) And that can stand in the path of reality just as much.

But done correctly, an outside perspective can offer you an accurate picture in the same way a mirror can, reflecting back the characteristics and qualities that shape your organization and its interactions every day, with every audience. In fact, a critical piece of advice we offer our clients is to invest part of their marketing research budgets in the task of building self-awareness. Of course, it's important to understand the competition. And it's vital to understand how prospective markets think. But without understanding what makes your organization go—what current customers (the "inner core" of our golf ball) love and what they dislike; what drives the staff (and what drives them crazy); what works and what doesn't—without understanding all that, you're missing a satellite, and a chance to find your real place in the market.

That having been said, we are also realists. We are aware that there are times when budgets shrink, and you will be forced to cut back to bare necessities. Even—or perhaps especially—in those times, it is critical that you not ignore the first-satellite question. So, even though our 20 years of experience suggest the value of securing outside assistance in the process of self-discovery (who knows what bell towers you're missing on *your* campus?), if you find yourself under constraints that won't allow you to do so, you can still work to understand your institution in richer and more meaningful ways.

...

In the following pages, we have included eight specific approaches you can implement to begin answering the first satellite question: "Who are we?" (Think of this as the "how to" of "who who.") Any of these techniques will get the job done. And you may want to employ more than one. In fact, over time, I'd suggest you try them all. Each will reveal your institution in a fresh and enlightening way.

1. Get to know your taxonomy.

You really don't have a brand—much less coherence—until you get to specifics. Only when you begin to describe yourself in very specific terms do you have any chance of finding a place in the mind of consumers. For example, "a liberal arts college in the United States" is not a brand. That's simply a genre. We have more than 500 institutions in the U.S. that classify themselves as liberal arts colleges. So, how can you find the specifics that set your institution apart from the crowd?

You may remember from high school biology that classifying plants and animals requires some ranking of information: domain/kingdom/phylum/class/order/family/genus/species. (One of our teammates remembers his teacher's brilliant mnemonic device for the sequence: **DO KEEP PONDS CLEAN OR FROGS GET SICK.** You will never have difficulty with this again.) These taxonomic rankings can serve as a great strategy for helping us discover who we are.

Interestingly, most institutions know their domain, kingdom, phylum and class well. But they often fail to go much beyond that.

Let's try an example, digging a bit deeper into the taxonomy of Warner Pacific College:

DOMAIN	Higher Education
KINGDOM	United States
PHYLUM	College
CLASS	Liberal Arts
ORDER	Tier 1 Western Region
FAMILY	Christian
GENUS	Church of God
SPECIES	Humanities Core/Paradox/Urban setting

Once we get to "family" in the list above, we start to articulate distinctiveness for Warner Pacific College. When we can describe a one-of-a-kind learning experience of four years at a top-tier Christian college in urban Portland, including a humanities core curriculum that helps students navigate the significant paradoxes of life, we just might connect with a student, a parent or a donor.

2. Get to know your background.

Remember Julie Andrews in *The Sound of Music?* (Another indication of my age.) When she taught her flock of children to sing, she taught them the scales. The first line of that infamous song begins, "Let's start at the very beginning, a very good place to start." And we'd suggest you start at the very beginning, as well. Read your history. What clues about your current identity are suggested by delving into your roots? Ask questions like: Whose idea was it to start our school? Why did they think it was important to venture into education? What did they hope to accomplish? What need were they fulfilling? How did they want to distinguish our school from others? Whom did they intend to serve? Why *this* place and time?

You will find amazing answers to these questions. You might discover that your church-related roots still have bearing on your decision-making. You could stumble upon a founder's sentiment that still holds forth today. You may find that the occasion of your founding implies significant values that you still espouse. Or you may be surprised to find that your ignoble history has yielded to very noble goals and causes. When we dive into their histories for our clients, we generally turn up valuable clues to determining specific messaging. Recently, on a site visit, we asked about the origins of the college's name. Interestingly, no one could tell us. Not the president, not the public relations director, not the admissions director. Not even trustees. We really had to dig. But we found it buried within historical documents, and that discovery yielded a powerful new message for the institution that helped audiences, both internal and external.

The moral? If you don't know much about history, start by studying yours.

3. Get to know your mission.

Now, just a few pages ago, we gave mission statements a pretty hard time. And we stand by our assertion that you will miss the mark if you believe your mission statement depicts the full, complex reality of your institution's identity. Nevertheless, a great mission statement does synthesize the highest purposes of your institution, and the outcomes expected from those purposes. So look for clues about how your mission statement informs everyday activity on your campus. Furthermore, most mission statements for colleges and universities include some beautiful, lofty language that stems from the emotional and spiritual (yes, spiritual) commitments of the founders of the institution and/or the writers of the mission. A great way to capture distinctive messaging about your campus is to return to this lofty language; there are no doubt gorgeous nuggets of lyrical genius in that flowery, 19th-century prose.

Peter Drucker says a mission statement should be brief enough to fit on a t-shirt[1]; but whether your mission statement is seven or seven hundred words, each was hopefully selected very carefully. Get to know why.

4. Get to know your stories.

Early in my career, when I managed the alumni program for my alma mater, one of my favorite activities was sitting with alumni of all ages and listening to their stories of their days at Spring Arbor. I learned volumes of valuable information that never found its way to the school's history book. Those stories enlightened me about the ways the University had influenced people and events around the world. A few important moments in the life of a student transformed people and places like the proverbial flapping of butterfly wings. Those stories had depth, meaning and passion. Collectively, they opened my eyes to the magnitude of Spring Arbor's great cause.

Thousands of thrilling stories distinguish your institution from all others. Hear them. Make an effort to find them. Write them down. Retell them. This is not difficult. Honestly, it will take some of your time. And your commitment to listen. But finding them is not an insurmountable task. Form a listening group with students or faculty. Take the theater department faculty to lunch. Have a cup of coffee with a sophomore. Attend an alumni gathering and sit with members from the Class of 1949 or '54 or '72. Just ask them to tell you how they arrived at your college. And how their experiences at your institution have influenced their life paths. Show up at homecoming events and butt in on conversations. Take a walk with the dean. And just listen. You will learn more than you imagine.

When we were conducting interviews prior to a capital campaign for a leading Catholic women's college, we noted that wearing the school ring was common custom for alumnae. So in our line of questioning, we began asking each participant to tell us what wearing the Saint Mary's ring meant to her. What did they think of when they saw it on their right hand? What memories did it prompt? What lasting influence did the ring represent? Among tear-filled responses, we found key opportunities for messaging to use throughout the successful campaign.

5. Get to know the experience.

If you are over 25 years old, you don't know what life is like for an 18-year-old freshman. Sorry, but it's true. You are, shall we say, out of touch. If you are over 30, you are, in fact, clueless. This requires that you get in touch with the experience of attending your institution today. You will not discover this by staying in your office. Nor by sitting in a chair reading this book. So put this down, and head over to the cafeteria for lunch. Go work out in the fitness center. Watch TV or play a video game in a residence hall lounge. Or stay up all night in the library. Sit through a boring lecture. Participate in a lively seminar. Run with the cross-country team, if you are able. You get the idea. Knowing your institution begins with everyday life on campus.

As we mentioned in the previous chapter, at RHB we employ *Circles of Influence*SM, our own qualitative research methodology, to get at the heart of the student experience on a given campus. We've also played pool in Roberts Wesleyan's student center, outbid for a great dinner at Guilford's student-run charity auction, swam in the Saint Mary's pool, attended chapel at Tyndale in Toronto, watched the GymDawgs at UGA, helped clean up Mt. Tabor with students at Warner Pacific, and watched basketball in Saint Joseph's Alumni Memorial Fieldhouse. Why have we engaged in the process like this, you ask? All with one ambition: getting to know the experience of attending these schools as authentically as possible. To get the real story, you have to go where the action is.

6. Get to know the language.

It's often told that Eskimos have 50 (or 75 or 100) words for "snow." Though all of those numbers are likely exaggerated, the idea is still circulated because it compellingly illustrates the concept that differences in language speak to differences in culture. Someone who lives in New Orleans, or New Delhi, wouldn't need specific terms for "wet snow" or "packed snow" or "drifting snow," because their everyday realities don't include those experiences.

Your campus has its own language, too, and that language is closely tied to the experience of attending your institution. Indeed, the particular turns of phrase that you hear around you can open an important window to your school's personality. Hearing Sweet Briar students describe themselves as "girls" is a prime example. So, too, is hearing about "the Hood hello" from nearly everyone you meet at Hood College—the creation and proliferation of this phrase speaking to the warmth and friendliness of the campus community. Likewise, if you visit Saint Joseph's University, you'll hear students campus-wide regularly reference *"cura personalis"* and "the *magis"*—indicating the degree to which the Jesuit ideals of "concern for the individual" and striving for excellence (or "the more") define the SJU experience, even for those students who are not Catholic.

Keep your ears open. The way your campus talks about itself may give you some valuable clues as to what makes you distinctive.

7. Get to know your traditions.

Hope College's annual Freshman Pull comes to mind. This isn't your run-of-the-mill tug-of-war. This is one muddy battle. And it's been going on for more than 100 years. This tradition is no nonsense. It influences the course of history. And it's what students and alumni remember with tears (and likely, mud) in their eyes. The College has an entire portion of its website devoted to Pull recollections from alumni, dating to 1898. That single tradition is a defining mark for Hope College. It's not the crux of the institution's exceptional educational experience, but it helps define who Hope is.

Your school likely has some funky ways of doing things, too. Don't fear them; acknowledge and embrace them. Your traditions, weird as they may be, distinguish you from all others and help shape your distinctive brand.

8. Get to know the relationships.

My brother-in-law, a noted psychologist and author, regularly reminds me "it's all about relationships." In fact, he gives out baseball caps with that phrase embroidered on the front. He suggests that in every way—physically, emotionally and spiritually—good relationships make us healthier, helping us live longer and more happily. He cites proof studies, literally hundreds of them, pointing to the importance of relationships.

What can I say? By understanding the relationships at work in your institution, you will be able to better answer the first satellite question. We encourage our clients to develop a relationship chart, a graph that shows how and with whom people interact in their organizations. Begin by understanding the interaction among employees. (An organization chart is one handy tool to acquaint you with this dynamic.) Then explore a bit more to see how offices, departments or work groups within your institution relate. How well does the advancement office interact with the academic dean? How often does the admissions director interface with the head of the career office? When do the athletic director and the alumni director have opportunity to discuss topics of mutual interest? While you are at it, chart out friendships between officers and offices. Who has whose ear?

Expand your chart by exploring how your customers interface with various offices and representatives within your institution. Where—and who—is your frontline with customers? You may be surprised to discover that your admissions office receptionist can be the most influential person on your campus.[*]

Finally, observe how your customers connect with one another. Which donors influence others? What roles do trustees and regents play? Who are the student leaders on campus? Which parents are the most vocal, and what effect do they have upon others? How do your customers communicate with one another? Simply observe by walking (or surfing) around. Ask direct questions. Find out what's happening under the radar that shapes your brand experience. After all, it's all about relationships.

...

Bottom line: Begin your exploration of the three satellites by answering the first question first: Who are you?

And remember: Pat answers aren't acceptable here. Your logo isn't who you are. Your tagline isn't who you are. The first paragraph of your viewbook isn't who you are. Your best features aren't even who you are. Until you can capture a full and honest assessment of your institutional identity, you won't achieve coherence. This is the starting point.

---

[*] At Lawrence University, this person bears the fitting title "Director of First Impressions." Clearly, the Lawrence team understands the value of the frontline.

---

1   Peter F. Drucker, *Managing the Non-Profit Organization*, HarperCollins Publishers, 1992

CHAPTER 8

Satellite Two: What on Earth Are You Saying?

Truth to tell, the task of accurately communicating about ourselves is just as weighted, freighted and tricky as the task of understanding ourselves in the first place. But if, as we've discovered, mission statements offer a reflection distorted by our highest callings and aspirations, our communications often secretly sell us short. Like a sagging hem in the back where you can't see it, or spinach on a tooth, our marketing communications have a million ways of betraying us and belying a polished appearance. Here are just three.

1. Creating white noise instead of buzz.

One of the most common—and, unfortunately, most deadly—marketing mistakes is sending too many messages. We don't mean too many pieces, we mean too many messages: "We're high-quality." "We're high-value." "We're high on our clients." "We're excellent stewards." "We'll hold your hand." "We offer S & H Green Stamps." "We're the best all-men's, technologically focused dental school in a suburban setting south of the Suwannee. And did we mention that we have night classes?"

Can you hear the static yet? Because your clients can. If you are trying to sell everything about your organization, all at once, your clients are hearing the white noise of too many marketing messages. What you want instead is buzz—that pleasantly tingling sensation that people are talking about you, and they're excited. Buzz comes from choosing marketing messages carefully and communicating about them effectively. It's not militantly sticking to one or two selling points, and it doesn't mean that you have to forego letting people know about all your strengths and long suits. But it does require you to have a savvy strategy that relates messages, to each other and to your audiences, effectively.

Not long ago, a friend e-mailed me immediately after having taken his daughter on a series of college campus tours. Though I didn't keep the e-mail on file, I believe his exact words were, "Rick, you've got to do something! Do you have any idea how horrible these tours are?" He told of how he watched his daughter's eyes glaze over at the irrelevant, scripted, almost-relentless speeches of the student tour guides—and how both father and daughter were mortified by the guides' "inside track" stories when they departed from the script. To Chris and his daughter, the blathering sounded like Charlie Brown's teacher. Thrill turns to chill when there's simply TMI—or at least too much *indistinguishable* and *insignificant* information.

One last word: Don't forget that white noise can arise from static in visual messaging, too. A few years ago, we were working with a campus on the important second satellite question *(what do we say we are?)* and discovered 28 different business card designs in use. Twenty-eight! Say nothing of the expense. Can you imagine the confusion caused by that unfocused imagery and lack of continuity? It was a complete and total buzz kill.

2. Selling the sand and not the shells.

Here's an incontrovertible truth: Your institution is genuinely one-of-a-kind. If it weren't doing something at least a little bit different from everybody else, it would have dried up years ago. Think of what you have to offer that no one else has as seashells— lovely things, each one an incomparable treasure.

But sometimes our clients are insecure about their seashells. Theirs don't seem as big as someone else's, or the colors are perhaps not as vivid, or some of the shells are chipped here and there. So they decide the seashells aren't worth peddling. Instead, they look around for another product, and they see sand, something that won't be so closely scrutinized, something available in copious quantities. The only problem is, everyone has sand. It isn't anything special, and it sure won't distinguish you from the competition.

The classic version of this among our clients comes from a small, private liberal arts college. Maybe it has a distinctive church affiliation. Or a sweet setting. Or a roster of programs that are off the beaten path. But it doesn't have a great big chambered nautilus, a single, gorgeous specimen that stops seashell-shoppers in their track. So, instead of polishing the shells it has, it sells the generic sand of

"We're friendly," "We give individual attention," and "Our professors post their office hours and even give out home numbers." And that's too bad…because the market for sand is perennially soft.

3. Sending Cinderella to the ball in tatters.

What made Cinderella a princess? Well, her heart and spirit, of course. But what got her noticed at the ball? A stunning gown and pair of drop-dead gorgeous glass slippers. While marketers of widgets and batteries have the unenviable task of sometimes putting a bow on a pig, we can say with complete conviction that our clients are truly some of the most beautiful and noble organizations you'll find anywhere. So, when they dress up, they become Cinderella—no less admirable in spirit, but often considerably easier on the eye.

Too often, colleges and universities rely on their wonderful work and excellent missions to sell their organizations. Their marketing materials reflect this shortsightedness, with well-meaning but lackluster copy, limp design and entirely too many lame, grip-and-grin photos. It's nothing that a magic wand and some enchanted mice (or barring that, creative energy, hard work and a solid investment) can't change. But it can spell the difference between scrubbing floors for an evil stepmother and spending happily ever after with a prince.

Several years ago, when we began our work at Goshen College, a Mennonite institution in northern Indiana, we were delighted by the energy and positive spirit we observed when conducting our on-campus research. Despite being mired in some gloomy enrollment patterns, the community approached life full of hope, faith, free-spiritedness and just enough healthy cynicism about "the mainstream" (including marketing) to keep things interesting. In fact, in one of our interviews, a faculty member described Goshen students as "joyfully maladjusted"—a description that seemed to wonderfully capture the vitality of the campus community. Goshen's completely distinctive climate and character made us eager to tell the stories we heard.

Yet, as we approached the second satellite question, examining the College's current communication efforts, we were disappointed to find its recruitment tools wrapped in dark colors, dull images, and a low-key, nearly morose tone that invited prospective students to hard work and service for an unjust world. While those messages are certainly part of the College's heritage and ethos, the whole picture was not being painted. "Aha," we noted, "this is *not* coherent. This is not telling the truth." The College's marketing materials were cloaking its Cinderella spirit in tatters, not telling a story of joy at all. Fortunately, Goshen was up for change.

We went to work on developing a more accurate rendering of the Goshen story. A new campaign, "The Joy of the Journey," described the one-of-a-kind experience awaiting prospective students. Bright colors, engaging photos, lively testimonials and a freshened website, along with dozens of other correlated improvements, all contributed to a revitalized image at Goshen. We also celebrated the slightly-off-center leanings that differentiate the College by tilting the "O" in "Goshen" a little to the left in an updated wordmark. (Not everyone "gets" that subtle message, but "insiders" wear it like a badge.) This willingness to embrace change paid off when, in the first year, inquiries rose by 90 percent, visits increased by 67 percent and matriculants rose by 45 percent. As you might expect, the campus began to embrace the new direction with "joy."

...

So how do you know if *your* institution has fallen prey to these traps and lapses? We encourage our clients to invest in a "coherence inventory": a thorough examination of their current marketing efforts, with an eye toward identifying missed opportunities, as well as successes upon which to build. This step is important, because you will discover avenues for better connecting with your audiences. And along the way, you may find some cost-saving measures, too.

Like the important task of learning more about your institutional identity, conducting a coherence inventory is usually easiest and most effective when completed by someone with an outside perspective—for a number of reasons. For one, you'd be surprised by how difficult this satellite really can become. In our experiences with hundreds of clients, this satellite causes the most stir. This is the point in our partnership when most of the institution's politics come into play, making it tricky for internal players to be completely open. After all, talented professionals in the organization have had a huge stake in the strategies and creative development of your communications and relationship building. And it's tough, particularly in an organization that prizes freethinking and creativity, to reign in well-intended efforts that may be missing the mark.

Second, but certainly related, it can be difficult for internal evaluators to keep the end goal in mind. And by this, we mean that it's easy to make excuses for the weaknesses you may disclose in the process. "We were short on money." "We needed this in a hurry." "This was so-and-so's first attempt." "The president's spouse really likes purple." "The history department chair has a neighbor/cousin/child who does graphic design, so she got this done for next to nothing."

However, in order to stay focused on the end goal of better connecting with your consumers, a coherence inventory must be completed while wearing "audience glasses." Your marketing efforts must be seen and evaluated, as best as possible, from the perspective of your constituents: students, prospects, donors, parents, patrons, benefactors, legislators. Each wears a slightly different lens prescription, so conducting the coherence inventory entails a fairly frequent change in frames. But in all cases, the focus must remain on the questions at hand: How would your constituents assess your efforts? Would they be forgiving? Indifferent? Or would they be dismissive? Remember, most of them don't know you, your marketing team, your president's spouse or your history chair's designer friend. And the majority of them don't yet have a relationship with your institution. None of this is to say that representatives of your school can't reach for "audience glasses" themselves; but the task of first prying off one's "insider's goggles" is an uphill battle for most of us.

Finally, conducting a coherence inventory requires a keen attention to that which you are doing *right*, as well as opportunities for improvement—and this can be difficult for internal players, too. As easy as it is to explain away shortcomings, it's equally easy to get so focused on the missteps that you're ready to throw the proverbial baby out with the bathwater. An external perspective can help you identify, celebrate, nurture and develop the areas of your communications tools and strategies where you're already succeeding.

But let's say that your institution has no internal politics (I'm chuckling as I type that), you're ready to trade your "insider's goggles" for some "audience glasses", and you're prepared to be as objective as possible—looking for both weaknesses and strengths— as you endeavor to answer the second satellite question of "Who do we say we are?" The next section provides some practical suggestions that will help you approach a second-satellite investigation with confidence and integrity.

...

What do we (or you, if you're giving this a go internally) look for in a coherence inventory? To begin, we check for accuracy, honesty and overlooked opportunities. Are we too modest? Are we over-stating a particular benefit? Are we hiding a really interesting seashell? This "message check" should be evaluated in terms of both design and copy, including content, layout, writing, photography, and all the myriad ways that messaging is conveyed.

We also identify gaps or redundancy of efforts. For example, if two or three departments on your campus have a need for a particular communications tool, you may be able to create one brochure, web page or template that can serve all three. Rather than each department fielding the cost for a brochure, the three can share the expense of one. In addition, we examine the continuity and consistency of communications (see page 77: 28 different business cards on one campus).

Finally, we look to see if messages relate appropriately, both to the audiences that are receiving them, and the media by which they're delivered. For example, will sophomores in high school really be captivated by (or even understand) the benefits of your independent-study senior capstone? If not, you might consider holding that message until later in your communication flow. Likewise, media and messaging should be closely linked. Why send text-heavy print messages to copy skimmers? Or, why invade cell phones with uninvited text messaging?

Remember: content matters most. Telling your story well to the right audiences at the right time and the appropriate way will yield an exchange satisfying to both parties. Misusing a medium—trying to build artificial community via social media sites, sending insignificant signals in your advertising, adding unnecessary volume to your website, for examples—will only de-fuse your dynamic message.

Above all, as you're answering the question, "Who do we say we are?," seek out opportunities. Remember what you learned in the first satellite. What are the experiences, stories and vivid descriptors that reflect you best? Are these showing up in your communication and marketing efforts? Are these stories being told? Use the second-satellite investigation to uncover the opportunities that will distinguish your institution from competitors, and help your audiences develop meaningful relationships with you. These rich opportunities will help you on your course toward coherence.

...

With those general objectives in mind, you're ready to begin your coherence inventory. Following are 25-plus questions that show up on our inventory list. This list is certainly not exhaustive, but it should give you a place to start.

25 QUESTIONS TO JUMPSTART YOUR COHERENCE INVENTORY

1. How consistent are the facts in our materials? (Do we say we have a 72-acre campus in one brochure and an 80-acre campus on our website? Our audiences may determine from that inconsistency that we are not certain, not careful or not to be trusted.) Are the facts we offer relevant to the audience?

2. How well are we identified in our communications? (Is our name prominent? Is it clear where these materials originated?)

3. How does our institution sign its name? What's our signature? (Are we consistent in delivering this important information?)

4. Is it clear how to contact or reach us? How easy and convenient is it to reach us? (Do we always use the same main address? Do we expect our customers to do more work to reach us than is necessary?)

5. Have we asked for a response? (What action do we want the readers to take?)

6. Have we invited our audience to a conversation? How often? (How much interest are we showing in the readers' responses?)

7. Do we use our official logos and wordmarks consistently and clearly? Would our audiences think so?

8. How many times do we use "you" language? "We" language?

9. What are the primary messages we are sending? Why? (Do we use language that is easily understood? Do we use jargon?)

10. Are our primary messages consistent with what we heard in our Satellite One study?

11. What communications tools do we employ? Are these methods appropriately matched to our audience(s)?

12. How well are we integrating our key messages across these media?

13. What is the user experience for our primary audience?

14. What is the user experience when someone visits our website? Receives materials in the mail? Visits us?

15. How do we treat guests?

16. How honest are we about our flaws? What do we say about our weaknesses?

17. What clues in our communications reflect our attention to our primary audience?

18. What messages and/or experiences are not being communicated well? What might we be communicating that we're not intending?

19. What opportunities exist for new user experiences? For new communications? For new marketing endeavors?

20. Do we have a "style," and is it consistent with our messaging? Is there more we can do with that "style"?

21. Are we saying the same things about ourselves across the board? (If a donor and a prospective student had a lunch conversation, would they be able to recognize our institution in the other's perspective?)

22. Do our mottos, taglines and campaign themes reflect our mission? Our key messaging?

23. What does our logo communicate about us? Is our logo sufficiently recognized to stand alone?

24. How well organized are our communication flow systems? Do messages follow a logical sequence?

25. How quickly are we able to respond to audience requests?

Remember: don't feel limited by this list. Ask your own important questions to explore what your institution is really communicating about itself.

What you say about yourself will have a significant bearing on what other people think—and say—about you.

CHAPTER 9

Satellite Three: Enough About Me. What Do *You* Think About Me?

For many agencies, marketing counsel starts with focus on external audiences, not the primary audience. It's all about what *others* think. Perceptions. Appearances. Smoke and mirrors. Image is everything.

You know, we've never liked what such a shallow perspective says about our marketing industry. Furthermore, we think—frankly— that a superficial take on marketing may come back and bite you in the ankle—especially if you're a college or university. As we've noted earlier, marketing is at its core a very simple thing, an exchange between two parties in which each has something the other wants. If you are always trying to second-guess or even outwit your exchange partner—to sell him what you think he wants, instead of what you are capable of delivering—you're not only going to make a mess of things with him, but you're also likely to earn a wider reputation for shady dealings. And, perhaps more to the point, our clients honestly have a great deal to offer in exchange. No need to bend the product to fit perceptions.

But just because we don't recommend a marketing strategy that is driven solely by external perception doesn't mean you can get by without knowing what outsiders think. Until we receive a signal from the third satellite, we're really only fooling ourselves into believing we know where we are. This third satellite signal provides information that is essential in at least two ways:

1. Understanding misperceptions

It's tempting to think of external audiences as an unruly preschooler. You can talk until you are blue in the face, and still not get through. You can sit this pugnacious tyke down and meticulously identify your organization's best qualities, carefully explaining their features and benefits, only to be told, "You smell stinky." You know it's the infuriating little imp himself who's the stinker; but what are you going to do?

The analogy certainly gets at the anger and futility that many of us feel in being faced with the seemingly impossible task of having to change someone else's screwy version of reality. And the analogy hints at another unfortunate truth as well: It doesn't matter that misperceptions are wrong. It only matters that someone thinks they're true. In marketing, as in golf, you have to play the ball where it lies.

But the analogy is wrong in one key way. Unlike headstrong toddlers, most of the audiences you need to reach as an educational institution do respond to reasoned arguments. They are rational. They may even be kindly predisposed toward your school or its work, or both. You *can* win these audiences over. But first you have to figure out where they have gotten off track in understanding what you do. And for that task, you need externally focused market research.

While we were working on the third-satellite study at Thomas More College, a Catholic liberal arts college in northern Kentucky, we discovered that most alumni wanted to be better connected to their alma mater but perceived a lack of interest on behalf of the institution. As disheartening as this misperception was, we nonetheless understood this finding as a pivotal opportunity for Thomas More. Indeed, the president and the marketing and advancement teams at the College embraced the challenge, and set to work in creating more occasions for alumni interaction and relationship-building. As a result, within two years, alumni giving had increased, and alumni involvement had skyrocketed, with Thomas More seeing an increase of 150 percent in alumni who returned to campus and became involved with the College in some way.

Misperceptions—frustrating, scary or discouraging though they may be—can lead to tremendous growth and progress.

2. Comparing yourself to the competition

We know. We know. Here's where market research gets scary. Considering how your institution stacks up against competing organizations—groups that vie for your audience's time, money or sympathies—is as nerve-wracking and potentially ego deflating as a junior-high dance. Will that special someone notice your shy charms, your keen wit, your true heart? Or will the object of your affections callously throw you over for someone whose assets are entirely physical and completely superficial? My palms get clammy just thinking about it.

But take heart. If you're still in business these days, you can be sure you are winning some hearts out there. Your audiences are finding plenty to like about you. Unlike at the big dance, you have the luxury of knowing that you can take on the task of measuring yourself against the competition without facing total rejection. And far more important, you'll gain insights and information you need to win over even more of your key constituencies. It's true that a great deal is at stake: increased donations, a growing reputation, a more qualified first-year class. But you can't lose by asking your clients, prospective clients, and even the competition for their frank opinions. You can only win. We promise.

There are even more reasons to undertake external research, but these are two of the most important. And as you proceed with your third-satellite investigation, what's important to keep in mind is that external research is not all about playing to your audiences. It's about understanding them. You want to learn about their preferences, their perspectives and their personalities. What do they understand, believe, know and feel about your institution? What are they saying about you? What do they tell their friends, if anything, about you? What would cause them to blog or Twitter about you—and what do they blog or Twitter about besides you? Your audiences will make choices about you based on how they respond to these (and many more) questions. That's why it's worth your time and investment to learn the answers.

...

Unlike the other two satellites, we can't supply suggested lines of questioning or sample market-research strategies that can be easily applied to all institutions. What you want to know, and from whom, are wholly dependent on your school's particular goals and circumstances. And only once you've settled on your objectives and audiences can you determine how to best collect data. You can survey some audiences broadly. Others will require personal interviews. You can answer some questions quickly, even using existing data you already have on campus. Other questions will require time and significant effort. The avenues to information you select will be varied, and they will stem from your specific lines, and audiences, of inquiry.

What we *can* offer here are two nuggets of counsel. First, your investigation into what others say (and think) about you should be heavily shaped by what you learned in Satellites One and Two. If you've discovered, for instance, that your student-development programs are wildly popular with your primary audience, but are under-promoted in your communications, that's clearly one topic you'll want to explore with external constituents. (Could this feature open up new markets of prospective students? Would donors be interested in funding further initiatives to build a national reputation?) Therefore, we recommend pursuing external research as the final step in the three-satellite process. Only when combined with information about your institution and its current messages do external perceptions help to put you on the marketing map.

Our second recommendation? Do not guess about what your audiences are thinking. Your guesses are founded on your perceptions, not your audience's. Higher education communities, as you well know, can be a bit insular. Despite our craving a strong worldview, our worlds can be pretty tiny. When we were assisting the University of South Florida with its third-satellite study, one of the areas of investigation included the needs, interests and perceptions of certain out-of-state student markets. We all had hunches about what the key themes among these audiences might be; we suspected, for instance, that the University's Tampa location would be a compelling feature for many, and that out-of-state tuition could be a concern. But nobody foresaw that one of the primary, self-reported interests among students looking at out-of-state schools would be an institution's proximity to a major airport. Sure, this seems obvious in hindsight, and no, the finding wasn't a total surprise. But the *degree* of importance for this particular issue was. So you'd better bet that USF included some airport-proximity messaging in its communications with non-Florida prospects—and fast.

All of this is to say: Do not rely upon guesses and intuition when assessing the third satellite. You'll miss out on some critical insights and important ah-ha moments. *Something* will surprise you. And enlighten you. And point you in the right direction.

Indeed, whatever it is that you discover by seeking the input of your constituents, you cannot find your way to coherence without the third satellite. The theory of navigational triangulation requires the input from a third perspective.

Don't skip this satellite. You will be lost without it.

CHAPTER 10

Connecting the Dots

So you're sitting on a mound of information. You've gained the Three Satellite perspective. You know who you are, what you say you are and what others say you are. Now what?

Now you burrow through that information, mining it for the gems of connection. You might find a lot of loose soil and a ton of rocks, but you'll also find quartz and diamonds amongst the depths of data.

The first satellite will tell you all about your *strengths*—where you are great. The second satellite, with its coherence inventory, will give you information about your *assets*—what you have on hand and what you've been telling everyone you have. And the third satellite will tell you about *opportunities*—what stories you can tell, and messages you can send, that will better inform or persuade your audiences.

Here's where it gets fun.

Make a list of the top five or ten findings from your discoveries in the first satellite investigation. These should be the vivid descriptors, key messages or features/benefits that define you. Hopefully, in this process, you've uncovered some interesting stories that document and give credence to your primary strengths. A few good questions to ask at this point are:

How is our list of strengths differentiated from those of our competitors?

Could our competition say the same things?

Do we have an "angle" or take on this that distinguishes us from others?

Adjacent to that list (you might need a big sheet of paper or a whiteboard for this), delineate the key findings from the second satellite. At this point, don't analyze your list in comparison to the first satellite; just identify the top messages that are being conveyed through your communication efforts. Ask yourself:

What are our current messages?

What are we broadcasting through the variety of our marketing efforts?

What are the top five or ten ideas that we promote about ourselves?

Next to that, list the top five to ten perceptions from external audiences you uncovered in your third satellite study. Here, you want to think in terms of the big picture. While each of your specific audiences may differ on some perceptions, you want to look for the commonly held perceptions across the audiences who orbit around you. You might ask:

What are the top five common denominators that most of our audiences believe about us?

What are we doing to reinforce or confound these perceptions?

Is there one audience whose perceptions diverge sharply from the others'—and if so, do we know why?

When you have these three lists in columns, begin to look for connections between them. For instance, maybe you've identified the diversity of your student body and faculty as a primary strength; you've seen that your marketing efforts highlight the benefits of learning with others from differing perspectives; and you've discovered that your audiences perceive you as an institution that provides a horizon-broadening education with a global perspective. Congratulations! You are being coherent. (At least on that front.)

Equally important, however, will be the points of disconnect you identify among these three columns, because they will represent areas of opportunity.

- You listed your strong suit as academic rigor, but your audience perceives you as a party school? *There's an opportunity to provide new evidence to shift perceptions.*

- You heard stories of your educational experience transforming the lives of your students, but your donor appeals focus on bricks and mortar? *There's an open door to connect with new donors.*

- You've always downplayed your off-the-beaten-path location, but students say the seclusion assists in both academic focus and community building? *There's a seashell you can polish.*

- Your messaging centers on themes of quality and excellence, but your audiences notice corner cutting in your budget-wise brochures? *There's an occasion to better align experience and messaging.*

- You lead with your stunningly beautiful campus in your pitches and publications, but are parents wondering if you're "just another pretty face"? Or worse, are they suspecting their investments—*a la* tuition payments—are being squandered on non-essentials? *There's a possibility for more effectively sequencing and/or segmenting your communications.*

What these examples all point to is the importance of knowing where you are currently positioned *before* you attempt to make a significant move. Indeed, our clients frequently discover that their current position in the higher education marketplace and where they hope to be are not the same place. But identifying their starting point—the one spot that they currently occupy in the higher-education universe—is an essential first step. Once we have that information, we can generate a roadmap of sorts to help our clients arrive at their desired destinations. But the route to point C is going to look different, depending on whether you're starting at point A or point B.

...

You might be thinking this all seems like a ton of work. And you are right: it is. But the benefits of being coherent clearly outweigh the effort. Don't believe us? Ask those who have gone through the process, done the hard work—and reaped the rewards. By the way, they'll also tell you that it's fun; it's a chance to make a real difference because you've moved strategically rather than laboring less wisely and less effectively.

CHAPTER 11

The Benefits of Coherence: In Others' Words

For years, I've heard clients speak about the advantages of coherence. I've heard their success stories. I have seen the light bulbs go on in the heads of presidents, enrollment officers, advancement professionals, professors and directors of all types. As they begin to practice coherence in their outreach endeavors, I've observed as they achieve the results they hoped for. I have seen their delight.

You should see it—or rather, hear it—too.

COHERENCE PROVIDES A CLEARER SENSE OF DIRECTION

"We don't want to be any of our competitors. We want and need to be Warner Pacific."

As president of Warner Pacific College, Dr. Andrea Cook brings to the institution a solid understanding of coherence.

She has employed the coherence model on three campuses since 1999. "The three satellites of perspective were critical to really finding and coming to terms with ourselves," she continues. "We were so insular, and this research gave us occasion for reflection on who we are. We'd have a meeting and look around the table and all say 'we're exceptional,' but not know what that meant. The research—and the clarity of comments—from all our audiences, internal and external, gave voice to what it meant for us to be exceptional."

"Early in the process, we had a conversation about the urban perspective. We hadn't given thought to what it meant to be in the city. We didn't own our place. Until this process, we took our freshmen orientation groups out to the country for a retreat. Now we traipse them around the city, opening opportunities to them and helping them acclimate to this wonderful asset. We've learned to be intentional about being here. We're living into this place."

"Coherence brings institution-wide focus," she summarizes. "It's easy to be more focused on individual interests in a college setting. Organizations historically run by guilds, like higher ed, are challenged by the 'silo nature' of these individual perspectives. Without clarity about who you really are, your message can be diminished to the lowest common denominator. Coherence gives such organizational clarity."

COHERENCE IS COST-EFFECTIVE

"We've met a number of important goals, and our campaign helped us do that," verifies Nancy McDuff, Associate Vice President for Admissions and Enrollment Management at the University of Georgia. "We've succeeded in meeting target enrollments in numbers, quality and diversity. But what has surprised me the most is how long we've used this campaign. I had no idea we could carry this as long as we have. I had been accustomed to changing course—and certainly recruitment materials—every few years. But the accuracy of the message and classic reflection of UGA has served us well over time. I'm not spending time, effort and resources on changing creative direction. I'm able to invest in projects I'd always had to put off. And the consistency helps build integrity. Our prospects aren't confused by our changing messages.

"So as an unanticipated benefit, I've been able to amortize the investment over a longer period of time. We've stretched this campaign twice the amount of time from previous campaigns—and we're still using it! That makes the investment in research and design so much more cost-effective."

COHERENCE GIVES CONFIDENCE

"It's a little difficult to recruit students to a women's college in the rural south these days," confesses Ken Huus, dean of admission at Sweet Briar College. "But coherence is a different way of thinking, a different way of doing business. We came to realize that we could do something different than we had been. We learned that we could trust prospective customers to make the right and educated decisions that were best for them. We could tell our story and trust them to measure its fit for them. It gave us courage.

"I have to admit that some faculty came along reluctantly, with comments like 'Well, it can't get worse, so let's see what happens.' But our message and campaign gives our team such confidence. And, fortunately, we had incredible and immediate response from our markets.

"At every college fair, it's not just prospective students who come to visit our table. It's our competitors and peers who are asking for samples of our materials. It's gratifying to hear, 'You guys have the best stuff out there.' I'm not sure we can quantify the value of our marketing campaign when it comes to the feedback from peers. Coherence has put us at the forefront, allowing us to tell our story with pride."

"We've got nothing to apologize for."

COHERENCE DIFFERENTIATES—AND UNIFIES

You've heard from the admissions dean. Here's what Sweet Briar's then-president, Betsy Muhlenfield[1], says:

"The whole 'girls' thing still bugs me (and faculty are not particularly thrilled with it). But, during the evaluation of the concepts, one of my senior administrators reminded me that I simply couldn't get 'Think is for Girls' out of my head. It's memorable. And it certainly does what it is supposed to. We will never slip into the androgynous look again."

"Some think the pink stuff doesn't look like business," she quips. "But I don't believe you can overdo this work. We've really embraced the message and style. The trustees have responded very well to what we've done. And we've used the look every which way from Sunday: banners lining the drive into campus, outdoor boards, fund-raising appeals...you should see the bookstore!"

"I was and am impressed with *Circles of Influence.* The research process got to the heart of what is at the heart of Sweet Briar College. *Circles* is innovative at trying to come at networks and webs from a completely different direction. And it yielded wonderful language we could all use. The process moved us toward a disinclination to focus on particular programs, but to get at the emotion and experience of being here, regardless of major. It gave a sense of what it is that the community attached to it feels about the place. Prior to that, the fight was always about which programs should be highlighted. I found this approach refreshingly honest.

"We're not the same place we were 20 years ago. And not the same college we were five years ago. But even though the College keeps changing, our students and alumnae are tracking with us. You got it right, so alumnae of every age find the message coherent with their experience."

COHERENCE IMPROVES RETENTION

By his own admittance, Bob Spatig, director of undergraduate admission at the University of South Florida is a disciple of coherence. "I've been schooled in coherence, so I really know how and why it works. It makes so much sense. It's so logical." Bob has used the coherence model in his work at Guilford College in North Carolina, at the University of Georgia, and most recently at USF.

"As a young institution, we want to project the image of our vision, but we still have to connect it with real perceptions of the audience. And what's great about the coherence process is that it's organic. It comes from within, and it's rooted in reality. If reality isn't in line with institutional aspirations, and you cannot bridge that gap, then you're in trouble. But taking a hard look is so helpful. Being specific and authentic in telling your story may, in fact, turn away customers who might have been captured by a more generic message, but how much of that do you really want?

"The three satellites, starting with *Circles of Influence,* gave us license to focus on messages that were important to undergraduates, messages that our administration didn't understand were more important to the customers. We still may not have university-wide coherence; but in admissions, we were able to focus on ideas and messages for students and their parents that help them experience USF in a way that surpasses their expectations. Likewise, this process gave University Marketing and Communications a line of messaging that was relevant. And the external research gave us a sense of perceptions to aid us in product enhancements, particularly with University housing.

"Despite the decline in our state's market size, we increased applications by 40 percent. Admits are down a bit, because we are able to shape our class by our selectivity. No doubt that we had effective strategies to increase our prospect pool without the coherence process. There are plenty of ways to do *that.* But I don't think we could get the students we have in the application pool, or yield, if we weren't delivering a message that resonated with reality. Messaging has been key for us, and we still rely on data and perspective we gathered through this process.

"At USF, we've turned the corner on retention. Since we've focused the message on students who fit USF, we're seeing greater retention and larger graduating classes. It's a little scary on the front end, but the long-term payoff is huge."

---

1   Muhlenfield retired from the presidency of Sweet Briar in 2009.

CHAPTER 12

The Opposite of Coherence

Go with me to Target® for a few minutes.

We've walked through the logo-laden door, grabbed a red shopping cart and headed toward sporting goods. (We're buying a tent.) The smart people at Target know that we are prone to be impulsive in our buying, so they ensure that we see lots of products en route to the back corner of the store. We have to maneuver our way past other specialty sections, including the featured sales items, candy, pharmacy and housewares. We pass all kinds of home accessories, sheets and towels, lamps and kitchen gadgets, and now we're passing through the vase and glassware aisle. You know how they put all those tchotchkes on the aisles so you can't miss them…

You with me? You can almost hear the Muzak, right?

So, we've got our cart and we're in the aisle with all the vases. Displayed on this endcap are all sorts of vases in glass, ceramic, plastic and even marble and metal. But as you pass these many and varied options, your eye is drawn to a sparkle on the bottom shelf, its source a beautiful crystal bowl featuring a cut-glass pattern that makes each facet glisten. Even the overhead fluorescent lights seem to bounce elegantly off the bowl. So you reach down to pick it up, and when you do, you notice a turquoise box with a white satin bow tucked behind the bowl. You recognize that box. It's a dead giveaway brand signal: Tiffany's®! And sure enough, you notice a little Target sign—small rectangle with red bar across the top and black block letters—that reads: "Tiffany Crystal Bowl $7.99"

What a find!

You're thrilled to find such a beautiful bowl at an amazing price. You're picking that up as fast as you can and placing it carefully in your red cart. You are about to make someone very happy.

But wait. You can't see it, but the rest of us can: that thought bubble above your head. And in it, whether you are conscious of it or not, is that Four Ps chart that we discussed in Chapter 3. The classic marketing model, it's a circle with four, little pie-shaped pieces, one each to represent Product, Price, Place and Promotion. And at this moment in Target, with the crystal bowl resting in your cart, you're rehearsing the Four Ps and starting to scratch your head a little. Incoherence is starting to creep in.

Here's what you're thinking as you work your way around those Four Ps:

Product: "This is a great bowl. It's beautiful. I'd love to own a Tiffany bowl. This will look great on the table."

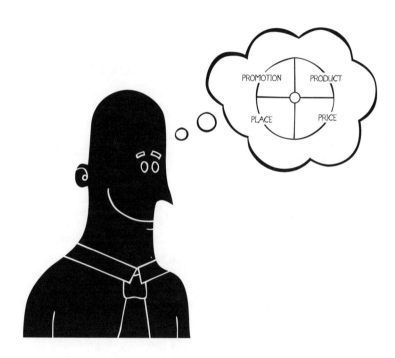

With every transaction, you and your customers process the 4 Ps.
Are you building trust—and coherence—with every transaction?

_____

_____

_____

_____

Price: "Hey wait...this is only $7.99. What a great buy. But aren't Tiffany bowls more expensive than that...like $799.00? Why is this one so cheap? What's wrong with it?"

Place: "And what's this doing at Target? Since when did Target start selling Tiffany? Isn't Tiffany more exclusive than that? And doesn't Target make Tiffany too accessible? Is Tiffany in financial trouble?"

Promotion: "Wouldn't this have been a big deal in the weekly circular? I didn't see it there. And wouldn't there be a big crowd lined up for these? How is it that there are any left? Why aren't they flying off the shelves?"

So, there you stand with your 4 Ps chart throbbing in your thought bubble, and you are concluding that things just don't add up: these facts are not coherent with what you believe to be true about Tiffany products. And you're starting to have second thoughts about your purchase.

You are behaving like most consumers. You are picking up on indicators of incoherence. And where there is incoherence, it's likely that marketing exchange will not take place. For eight bucks, you could—and might—take home the bowl in your Target shopping cart (especially in a tight economy). But you will always doubt it is a real Tiffany bowl. You might even return it a few days later. Even more likely, however, is that after contemplating the purchase, you take the bowl from the cart and put it back on the shelf.

Because of the doubt and mistrust bred by incoherence, you walk away from the exchange.

...

Of course, the importance of your achieving coherence far supersedes the value of a tchotchke in Target. The big point of this book is not about selling a bowl. Or simply selling your school.

I'm thinking about a young, Portland, Oregon, basketball player whose personal background negated some access to the higher-education opportunities he deserved. The practice of coherence at Warner Pacific College gave him an open window not only to a fine education, but also to the support and interest of a faculty who encouraged him to develop his natural capabilities to learn and lead. Had Warner Pacific not aligned its programs with its distinctive location, had the College not chosen to reduce tuition by more than a third to provide greater accessibility, had it not retained a coach with a heart for the young men of Portland—had it not chosen to embrace coherence—that young man and that institution would not have connected. And I'm thinking about 250 Warner Pacific students at work serving their neighbors and community. I'm picturing them improving the landscape of the city park, painting elementary school classrooms, tutoring children. Who can measure the significance of those lives, and the results of the important connections forged between those students and institutions and communities?

Or what about the young, African-American high schooler who is contemplating attending UGA? What if she were not to attend a campus-visit event where an admissions counselor specifically emphasizes the University's full commitment to supporting a diverse community? What if she were not to hear that counselor illustrate "our community is stronger with the voices of many" by leading the packed auditorium in a unified, electrifying roar of UGA's "calling the Dawgs" cheer? Would she have walked away from the exchange—missing the opportunity to study in UGA's extraordinary journalism (or genetics or business) program? Would UGA have missed out on her ideas, leadership and other community contributions? And, years later, how many lives might not be touched by her reporting (or healing or innovation)?

...

The reason I am so passionate about the coherence model—indeed, the reason I have written this book—is because the opposite of coherence isn't simply incoherence. It's missed opportunity. Unreached potential. Lost possibilities. Not only for your institution, but also for every individual your institution affects, or could affect, now and in the future, through its incredible reach. The idea of such enormous waste is distressing to me; it runs counter to everything I believe in.

But like the schools you've read about in these pages, you, too, can have record enrollments. Your annual fund and capital campaigns can be over the top. Your alumni can participate and volunteer more. Your trustees can be happier. Your legislators can be more supportive. Your name can be better recognized. You can achieve your goals. You can flourish, even in a dark economy. And your institution can be what it was meant and destined to be. You can change lives. Not just one or two. Thousands.

So, who's the student or parent or neighbor to whom you've

not yet told your amazing story? How will you shift your thinking in order to thrive as an institution? And how will you adapt to help your constituents thrive, as well?

Whose life will be changed forever because of what you do—and the fact that you do it coherently?

EPILOGUE

What's Next?

The conversation in the RHB conference room that launched our development of the model outlined in this book began with a question I posed to our team: "What's next?"

Times and circumstances were changing. The market was shifting. Communication was being transformed by digitally driven technologies. Consumers were gaining power, and we began wondering out loud: Given the diminishing strength of brands and their clear disconnect with our not-for-profit clients, what would be the next phase of consumer behavior and marketing exchange?

Since that time, and since beginning work on this book, the world experienced a collapse of the financial pillars on which we all built our hopes—and retirement funds. Colleges and universities, like most everyone else, have all been dealt a blow. Yet, what you have in common with everyone who has suffered the consequences of this seismic change is an opportunity to re-examine how you'll move forward; to rebuild, rethink, rework and reinvent; to reconsider how to be more coherent; to decide how you'll be ready for what's next.

This much is certain: In the worst economy in nearly 100 years, you must provide sufficient rationale for existence. In a word, you must differentiate. Clearly, genuinely, openly. You must provide a convincing case for your enormous cost. You have to prove the merits of your approach. You need to show the outcomes that make you a superior choice.

Further, you have to deliver on the experience. Like it or not, we live in an age where consumers simply won't put up with unresponsiveness; they have too many alternatives (including the burgeoning market of for-profit providers).

You have to do what you say you do. Be who you say you are.

And if your institution is to survive, you will deliver more than you promise. You'll be the one who listens, engages and speaks openly and honestly with your audiences. You'll be the one who becomes naturally transparent.

You'll be the one who practices coherence.

Recommended Reading

Adamson, Allen P. 2006. *BrandSimple: How the Best Brands Keep It Simple and Succeed.* New York: Palgrave Macmillan.

Anderson, Chris. 2006. *The Long Tail: Why the Future of Business Is Selling Less for More.* New York: Hyperion.

Baskin, Jonathan Salem. 2008. *Branding Only Works on Cattle: The New Way to Get Known (And Drive Your Competitors Crazy).* New York: Business Plus.

Beckwith, Harry. 1997. *Selling the Invisible: A Field Guide to Modern Marketing.* New York: Warner Books.

Bedbury, Scott and Stephen Fenichell. 2002. *A New Brand World: 8 Principles for Achieving Brand Leadership in the 21st Century.* New York: Viking.

Briggs, Rex and Greg Stuart. 2006. *What Sticks.* Chicago: Kaplan Publishing.

Cohen, Adam. 2002. *The Perfect Store: Inside Ebay.* New York: Little, Brown and Co.

Collins, Jim. 2001. *Good to Great: Why Some Companies Make the Leap...and Others Don't.* New York: Harper Business.

Drucker, Peter F., Jim Collins, Philip Kotler and others. 2008. *The Five Most Important Questions You Will Ever Ask About Your Organization.* San Francisco: Jossey-Bass.

Du Plessis, Erik. 2005. *The Advertised Mind: Ground-Breaking Insights into How Our Brains Respond to Advertising.* Virginia: Millward Brown.

Gerzema John and Ed Lebar. 2008. *The Brand Bubble.* San Francisco: Jossey-Bass.

Gilmore, James H. and B. Joseph Pine. 2007. *AUTHENTICITY: What Consumers Really Want.* Boston: Harvard Business School Press.

Heath, Chip and Dan Heath. 2007. *Made to Stick.* New York: Random House.

Kelly, Lois. 2007. *Beyond Buzz: The Next Generation of Word-of-Mouth Marketing.* New York: Amacom.

Kim, W. Chan and Renee Mauborgne. 2005. *Blue Ocean Strategy: How to Create Uncontested Market Space and Make the Competition Irrelevant.* Boston: Harvard Business School Press.

Lindstrom, Martin. 2005. *Brand Sense: Build Powerful Brands Through Touch, Taste, Smell, Sight and Sound.* New York: Free Press.

Neumeier, Marty. 2006. *The Brand Gap (Revised Edition): How to Bridge the Distance Between Business Strategy and Design.* California: New Riders.

Neumeier, Marty. 2007. *ZAG: A Whiteboard Overview.* California: New Riders.

Pine, B. Joseph and James H. Gilmore. 1999. *The Experience Economy: Work Is Theatre & Every Business a Stage.* Boston: Harvard Business School Press.

Ries, Al and Jack Trout. 2001. *Positioning: The Battle for Your Mind.* New York: McGraw-Hill.

Roberts, Kevin and A. G. Lafley. 2005. *Lovemarks: The Future Beyond Brands.* New York: powerHouse Books.

Sernovitz, Andy. 2006. *Word of Mouth Marketing: How Smart Companies Get People Talking.* New York: Kaplan.

Shirky, Clay. 2008. *Here Comes Everybody.* New York: Penguin Group.

Silverstein, Michael J. 2006. *Treasure Hunt: Inside the Mind of the New Consumer.* New York: Penguin Group.

Solomon, Robert. 2008. *The Art of Client Service.* New York: Kaplan.

Steel, Jon. 1998. *Truth, Lies, and Advertising: The Art of Account Planning.* New York: John Wiley & Sons.

Tisch, Jonathan M. and Karl Weber. 2007. *Chocolates on the Pillow Aren't Enough: Reinventing the Customer Experience.* New York: John Wiley & Sons.

Trout, Jack. 2001. *Big Brands Big Trouble: Lessons Learned the Hard Way.* New York: John Wiley & Sons.

Zyman, Sergio and Armin Brott. 2002. *The End of Advertising As We Know It.* New Jersey: John Wiley & Sons.

Coherence: How Telling the Truth Will Advance Your Cause (and Save the World) is printed on 55lb natural paper supporting the Sustainable Forestry Initiative. The text type in this book is set in Stone Print Roman, a "green" typeface in that it uses less space than most faces without sacrificing legibility. Sumner Stone designed the font in 1993. Stone Type Foundry is located on Alphabet Farm in Rumsey, California. The main text is supported by the legible sans serif font, Trade Gothic Condensed, created in 1948 by Jackson Burke, a book and type designer in California.

Kerry Prugh, senior art director at Richard Harrison Bailey/The Agency, designed the cover and book content. Her colleague, Brian Ross, art director at Richard Harrison Bailey/The Agency, created the illustrations.

Visit us online at coherencethebook.com